Bona Fide

Discovering your Leadership Locus

By F.R. Blass

Lusory Publishing

Contents

Author's Note

"Bona fide: Genuine. Sincere. Made in good faith without fraud or deceit."

—Merriam-Webster [1]

The motivation to write this book was born of necessity. Having been a college professor teaching leadership for over twenty years, I was never satisfied with available texts on the subject. Not that they were not quality books, on the contrary, some such as Gary Yukl's *Leadership in Organizations*[2] or Lee Bolman and Terrence Deal's *Reframing Organizations*[3] have had immeasurable influence on contemporary leadership thought. But I wanted something different in my class. I wanted my students to discover leadership as a complex, loosely defined, yet critical concept. Teaching mostly undergraduate students, context has always been a challenge when discussing leadership theory. How can I expect students who have never worked in an organizational setting to appreciate its nuances, especially those from a leader's perspective? To merely lecture about leadership theories, invariably reduces the conversation to an exercise of memorizing and regurgitating.

I wanted more than just monologue lectures with presentation slides, I wanted students to grapple with the complexity of leadership. So, I chose not to use a textbook and instead decided to write essays on topics which I felt were central to any conversation on leadership, and especially one on bona fide leadership. Class consisted of discussing the essays – period. I wrote the essays about already familiar topics (i.e. trust, humor, relationships, etc.) and tried to show how they were relevant to remaining authentic while answering the call to leadership. This book is a collection of those essays.

The essays were designed to examine just a few of the more salient and essential elements of leadership. Topics such self-presentation, trust, humor, sense-making, power, influence, persuasion, social exchange, empathy, politics, followership, and ethics were all presented in relative isolation to allow for examination; but in reality, leadership is a swirling, messy, interacting, blending, compounding of all of these factors and more.

I would have the students read the essay before class and then we would just talk about it. Over the years I added new topics at the urging of my students, but in general the course was organized around understanding yourself, understanding others, and understanding the situation. I called this the SOS approach to leadership. SOS is a call, and it is influenced by the leader (*Self*), who mobilizes *Others* to take action to address the *Situation* at hand – SOS. This SOS approach to leadership is quite similar to the ideas associated with the concept of "authentic leadership."

The concept of authentic leadership emerged from the field of positive psychology, and emphasizes how leaders can inspire others to follow by being true to who they are (rather than trying to emulate the behavior of others) and through the fidelity of their behaviors.[4, 5] While this book is not a book on authentic leadership, nor is it a book on leadership theory, the themes and discussions are more closely aligned with authentic leadership than with any other approach or leadership theory.

This is not a new approach to leadership – in fact, in the classic military strategy book *On War* written by Prussian general Carl von Clausewitz, he wrote of the genius of leadership during the Napoleonic wars in the early 1800s [6]. This "genius" was defined as being a very highly developed mental and psychological aptitude. According to Clausewitz, all of those gifts of mind and temperament, in combination, constitute the essence of military genius. Clausewitz proposed that military genius consists of a harmonious combination of elements, in which one or the other ability may dominate, but none may be in direct conflict with the rest. He cited intellect, *coup d'oeil* (the inward eye), *courage d'esprit* (moral courage), presence of mind, energy in action, strength of mind or character, and a sense of locality (imagination), as the elements of military genius.

There are various contemporary theories and models of authentic leadership consistent with Clausewitz's thinking, but perhaps the most noted is the one proposed by Bruce Avolio and William Gardner at the inaugural summit on authentic leadership hosted by the University of Nebraska-Lincoln's Gallup Leadership Institute in 2004.[6] In the subsequent *Leadership Quarterly* article on the same summit, they proposed that authentic leadership consisted of four primary components: *self-awareness* (self), *self-regulation* (which is also referred to as an "internalized moral perspective"), *relational transparency* (others), and *balanced processing* (situation).

Consistent with Clausewitz's ideas on "genius" and in line with the tenets of authentic leadership, this book is organized around three broad themes: introspections (self), intersections (others), and perspectives (situation). In the Introspections section, we will explore a range of topics that illustrate the complexities of social behavior and how we can better understand ourselves and others, with discussions on topics such as "Symbolism and Communication," "Making Sense and Learning," "Personality," "Empathy," "Humor," and "Emotions and Self-Presentation." While each subject is presented individually, they should be viewed as a tapestry. Something they all have in common is they are an attempt to gain insight into why we behave as we do. The implication is that if we can understand what makes us who we are, perhaps we can then better understand others.

In the Intersection chapters, we move into the social space and explore the interactions we have with others. Discussions on topics such as "Managing Impressions," "Understanding Social Roles," "Personal Reputation," "Trust and Social Exchange," "Interpersonal Relationships," "Social Capital," "Persuasion," and "Social Power" examine the dynamics that occur as people come together to accomplish tasks and compete for resources and opportunities.

Finally, in the Perspectives chapters, we look at organizational behavior through different perspectives in an attempt to better "see" the milieu we are in. Chapters that examine perspectives such as "Culture," "Dramaturgy," "Politics," "Followership," "Ethics," and "Leadership" each reveal different aspects of what it is like being a part of the social system that is an organization.

It is a fundamental premise of this book that being a good leader is much like being a good person. Good leaders inspire us, they elicit trust, they are fallible, show good judgement, have a sense of direction, and they get us to *choose* to follow them – they are bona fide. Being a *bona fide* leader, like being a good person, means you must know yourself, know and understand others, and "see" situational dynamics.

While the chapters are arranged to build on one another, they can still stand alone as well. Each chapter begins with a quote or two designed to prime the reader for the discussion that follows. At the conclusion of each chapter is a short story designed to illustrate the topic covered in the chapter. Following each short story are a series of *reflections* which are simply questions designed to foster deep thinking.

This book mostly reflects my understanding of others' great thinking and research. I have stood on the "shoulders of giants" both in the classroom and in writing this book. I chose to write it in a narrative style rather than a scientific one in an attempt to remain true to my original purpose: the creation of a rich educational resource on the topic of leadership. Every effort has been made to give credit where credit is due, and any omissions to that effect, are mine alone.

Finally, I'd be remiss not to mention my inspiration for the notion of bona fide leadership. I have had the privilege to observe and study leaders and leadership for most of my professional life. I have been influenced by countless men and women who answered the call to leadership, and the one thing they all have in common is that they answered the call.

References

1. *Merriam-Webster Dictionary.* [cited 2019 Web Page]; Available from: https://www.merriam-webster.com/.
2. Yukl, G.A., *Leadership in organizations.* Eighth edition, global edition ed. 2013, Boston: Pearson.
3. Bolman, L.G. and T.E. Deal, *Reframing organizations.* 5. ed. ed. 2013, San Francisco, Calif: Jossey-Bass.
4. George, B., *Authentic leadership : rediscovering the secrets to creating lasting value.* 1st ed. ed. Warren Bennis signature series. 2003: Jossey-Bass.
5. *Leadership: Theory and Practice, 8th Edition.* 2018, Ringgold, Inc.
6. Avolio, B.J. and W.L. Gardner, *Authentic leadership development: Getting to the root of positive forms of leadership.* The Leadership Quarterly, 2005. **16**(3): p. 315-338.

INTRODUCTION

Echoes from Childhood

"Adolescence is a critical period in human development... [it] is a time of experimentation, and choices made at this age can have enduring consequences."

—Sarah Hampson, Psychologist[1]

"The research of sociologists, anthropologists, and psychologists observing American children at play has shown that, although both boys and girls find ways of creating rapport and negotiating status, girls tend to learn conversational rituals that focus on the rapport dimension of relationships whereas boys tend to learn rituals that focus on the status dimension."

—Deborah Tannen, Linguist[2]

As we examine the various topics in this book, we will be attempting to better understand our behavior and the behavior of others. In doing so, we will be making attributions or assigning reasons to those behaviors. These attributions will range from dispositional ("What characteristics make that person do what they do?") to situational ("What is it about the situation that makes that person do what they do?") Interestingly, if you break it down to these perspectives, there would be little or no free will at the extreme end of each. Consider that if we assume individual characteristics alone explain all behaviors, then all of our actions are perfectly predictable and we lack free will; on the other hand, if situational forces explain all behaviors, then our actions are solely determined by external variables and as such we lack free will because we had no part in controlling what happened. It is therefore at the intersection of the two that we find the greatest free will and where we can assume that we have the greatest control of our own behavior and the greatest opportunity to influence the behavior of others.

We will explore that range in between the extremes and pay particular notice to the middle zone where the social influence zone exists (Figure 1). In this zone, we assign attributions to the behavior of others, fully aware that the dispositional and situational characteristics are engaged in a constant tug of war in our minds, and conscious that if we are not rigorous in our reasoning we can easily fall into the trap of biased thinking.

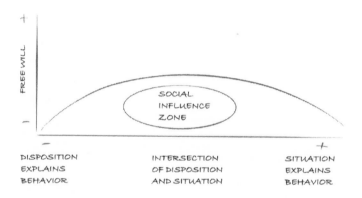

Fig
ure 1: Attribution Continuum

The term "fundamental attribution error," which was first coined by Larry Ross in 1977, refers to a common mistake made when making attributions.[3] This bias occurs when we use shifting perspectives to explain behavior. For instance, when I attribute the successes in my life to dispositional factors (i.e., industrious, intelligent, persistent), and the failures I experienced to situational factors (i.e., unlucky, lousy economy, poor timing). What is interesting about this common bias is that we tend to reverse it when assigning attributions to others. I attribute the successes in your life to situational factors (i.e., lucky, good economy, good timing) and the failures to dispositional factors (i.e., lazy, unintelligent, quitter).

So, with that caution, let's consider why we behave as we do. What makes one person fearful of talking in front of groups and another excited at the prospect. Why are some of us assertive and others passive? Are these personality traits that we were born with, or are these learned behaviors – or perhaps a combination of both?

Consider that adult social behavior is often reflective of salient childhood experiences and those experiences were encoded as memories by a child's brain. So, some may be magnified or distorted accordingly. Our adult perceptions of ourselves, our perception of others, how we behave in relationships, how we trust – essentially how we exist socially – are largely shaped and influenced by these recorded experiences during our childhood. It was through mostly trial and error, and while interacting with other children and adult authorities, that the foundation of our adult social psyches became imprinted. It is from our childhood socialization experiences that our sense of self-identity was determined, that our fears and inhibitions were learned and imbedded. Our childhood experiences shape how we perceive others and influence the stereotypes and biases we use to filter social stimuli. In sum, our childhood was an immersion experience in social experimentation and social learning.

Scientists studying human social development often cite "social learning theory" to explain how people learn and develop complex social behaviors. Based on the research of Albert Bandura, the theory contends that all social learning occurs as people interact with one another.[4] He argued that we learn through observing and communicating with others, and that we realize certain rewards and sanctions based on our behaviors. Relative to adults, children have a rather simple array of social behaviors, so according to social learning theory, children are constantly seeking cues on how to behave. As they observe others and witness rewards and punishments, or are told about them, they adjust their own behaviors to better align with the positive feedback and avoid the sanctions. As they learn from others and their own experiences, their behavioral sophistication increases.

Bandura stated that four necessary conditions must be present for effective social learning to occur: *Attention, Retention, Reproduction,* and *Motivation.* Attention refers to what is observed and varies depending on the amount of attention paid. This variation depends on a host of variables such as distinctiveness or saliency of observed behavior, attractiveness, prevalence, complexity, functional value, etc. In other words, our personal characteristics (observation skills, sensory capacities, degree of surprise, interest level, perceptual skills, previous experiences) all affect what we pay attention to.

Retention is retaining or remembering what you paid attention to. In order to reproduce an observed behavior, it must be stored in memory and be retrievable. Observers must be able to remember specific features of the behavior. This recall includes invoking the use of symbols, mental images, mental mapping, comparisons, etc. Consider a surprise. When we are surprised by a behavior, we obviously notice it. It stands out from other expected behaviors. It stands in contrast to what we expect, so it catches our attention. As we consider it, we must make sense of what we have observed in order to understand and retain it. Then we must put it somewhere for future reference, so we add the new information to our existing mental map for future retrieval.

Reproduction is replication of the observed behavior. This includes retrieving the stored information and then re-enacting it. There are many behaviors that we observe frequently, yet are unable to replicate. Often we are limited by our physical abilities and for that reason, even if we desire to reproduce the behavior, we cannot. For most of us, just watching someone play the guitar does not translate to being able to play the guitar.

Assuming we have the ability, we still must be motivated to reproduce the behavior. Yet, even with the motivation present, if we perceive that the costs outweigh the rewards, we are not likely to imitate the behavior.

To better understand this, we can turn to a theory that was formulated to explain human behavior, known as "expectancy theory." Expectancy theory was first proposed by Victor Vroom in his 1965 book *Motivation in Management*.[5] Vroom wanted to better understand the motivation behind why people chose to behave the way they do. He proposed that individuals choose to act in a specific manner because there is an expectation that the chosen behavior will result in a desired outcome. Similarly, Vroom proposed that individuals will choose to not act in a particular manner if they expect the behavior will result in an outcome that is not desirable. However, the motivational force behind expectancy theory is more than just the pursuit of a desired outcome. Vroom argued that in addition to the desired outcome, which he called *valence*, there were also the variables of *expectancy* (the expectation that a specific behavior will lead to a specific outcome) and *instrumentality* (the belief that the behavior is within one's capability).

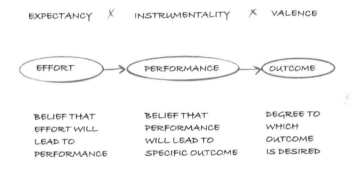

Fig

ure 2: Expectancy Theory

The expectancy theory of motivation has become a widely used theory in behavioral science and is particularly useful in helping us to understand the motivational process behind how individuals make choices about their behavior. From a social learning and modeling perspective, a decision to reproduce (or avoid producing) an observed behavior is dependent on the motivations and expectations of the observer.

Once an individual is motivated to reproduce a behavior, it is retrieved from storage, and behavior reproduction occurs. This requires a degree of cognitive skill, and in some cases requires physical skill and agility. Regardless, it involves reproducing the image of the behavior, including any physical capabilities, and self-observation of the reproduction. Observation and feedback from others can further enhance success. We will discuss this in much greater detail later.

A central component in Bandura's social learning theory is the idea of "reciprocal determinism." Reciprocal determinism is the notion that an individual's actions, the social environment they are in, and their personal characteristics, all come together to create a triad of influences with each one reciprocally influencing the other two.

Consider this: as children find themselves faced with new social environments, they must quickly observe, learn, and navigate those new environments to become socially comfortable. What they see is crucial to their understanding. Think of a child at a new school. Who am I? What are my strengths and weaknesses? Who are they? Who are the nice kids? Who are the not so nice kids? What is the teacher like? Who are the other authority figures? Who can be approached, who cannot? What are the norms for behavior at this new place? How do they react to my actions? How well do I get along on the playground? What are the sanctions for wrong actions? What are the rewards for right actions? The child must consider which groups or games can or cannot be joined, or perhaps more importantly, which ones *should or should not* be joined?

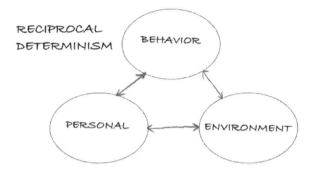

RECIPROCAL
DETERMINISM

BEHAVIOR

PERSONAL

ENVIRONMENT

Figure 3: Bandura's Reciprocal Determinism

Once children become a part of the new environment, they discover who *they* are within that environment. What is socially right and what is socially wrong? Children at play come to discover that what is socially right is what generally makes them or others feel good, and that what is socially bad generally makes them or others feel bad. Indeed, they become a part of the system and become the models that others emulate. How they are treated by others, and how they themselves treat others results in felt emotions that become the stimuli for learning.

Consider the childhood game of Follow the Leader. In Follow the Leader, one child has the role of leader and all the others must follow for the game to work. The leader then chooses a path around the playground or yard. Over benches, under fences, and through bushes, the leader revels in the trail of others following their every step. The leader's revelry is short-lived as others await their turn in the coveted position. As the next leader assumes the piloting role, the previous leader falls to the back of the line in hopes that another opportunity to lead will arise before attention is diverted to another game. If the former leader chooses not to follow, the game breaks down. Those who were awaiting their turn will be disappointed at losing their turn and may choose to start another game with others or continue without the former leader.

As with Follow the Leader, sometimes childhood play is fun, but other times it is the scene of disappointment or conflict. Countless questions are posed and answered in a child's mind daily. What are the rules of good play? What happens to kids that don't play by the rules? How are the rules of play learned? What determines in-groups and out-groups? Who are the leaders? Who are the followers? What are the behavioral norms? How are those norms different for males and females? Over time these questions get answered, although not always correctly. Rewards and sanctions quickly communicate the implicit rules. Leadership and followership are co-discovered through social interaction.

It is through socializing with others that children first learn that they act differently around different people and that others do the same. They also learn that their behavior is further adjusted when a third person joins the interaction. They learn that they can be accepted by more kids and have more friends if they are willing to act a bit differently depending on who they are interacting with. They learn that being their "true self" can earn some friends, yet lose others. They learn that to avoid conflict, they must sometimes behave in a manner not absolutely true to their being. Sometimes they must act cooler, funnier, tougher, or more sensitive, than they actually feel to create the social effect they desire.

This discussion is not intended to assert that all social learning occurs in childhood – on the contrary, social learning occurs continuously throughout life. What is important to note here is that early social learning is foundational in how we understand ourselves and others as adults, and therefore is an important place to begin when trying to understand social behavior.

As we examine who we see ourselves to be, we integrate our life experiences into a coherent whole. Some of these experiences become the ones that define how we like to think of ourselves and others define how we do not wish to be. Regardless, the experiences from our childhood are largely un-erasable and irrepressible. They are echoes from our past. They are the voices of our friends and enemies that we interacted with every day. They are the shadows in our adult minds that influence our behavior for the rest of our lives.

Deborah Tannen, a noted scientist specializing in linguistics and interpersonal communication has even asserted that the very manner in which we communicate as adults is imbedded with gender norms that were socialized into us as children.[2] She argues that when we communicate, these learned norms tend to place us in a "one-up" or "one-down" position depending on who we are communicating with. She suggested that males are socialized at a young age to learn to use language intended to establish one-up positions and young females tend to be socialized to use language that places them in one-down positions. These social reinforcements serve to imbed gender roles into the impressionable psyches of children that are manifested in adult behavior.

The rest of this book is devoted to exploring various aspects of how we influence others and how they influence us. As we explore these topics, we should be ever-mindful of who we are, who others are, and the myriad of forces and life experiences that come together to create the complex social systems within which we exist and that define our social existence.

Being a bona fide leader requires that we own who we are, and that includes our unique history. This is not to imply that we adopt a *que sera sera* attitude, indeed we should always be learning, growing, and refining our personas. Rather, we should examine our biases, recognize when and where we take cognitive shortcuts, and what criteria we use for taking those shortcuts. We should recognize that many forces have shaped who we are, and serious introspection can reveal blind spots that we would otherwise not even be cognizant of.

The following short story provides an example of the richness of those early social experiences and what may be learned from them. After reading the story, take a moment to reflect on the questions that follow.

Blue Eyes/Brown Eyes

In the book *A Class Divided: Then and Now* by William Peters, he tells the story of Jane Elliott, who at the time (1968) was a third-grade schoolteacher.[6] Elliott was struggling with how to discuss Dr. Martin Luther King's assassination, which had happened just the day before. She felt that mere words were inadequate to explain the tragedy and racial discrimination to her all-white third-graders. After the class arrived and settled in, she asked them if they understood what it might feel like to be a black boy or girl. She suggested to the class that the only way to truly understand discrimination was to experience it and suggested they try an exercise that would demonstrate it. The children were excited to participate.

At the beginning of the exercise, she determined that the blue-eyed children would be the discriminating group and brown-eyed children would be the discriminated group. She crafted special brown fabric collars and asked all of the "blue-eyes" to place them around the necks of the "brown-eyes" so that they could be easily identified. She then let the class know that the "blue-eyes" were to have extra privileges, such as extra food at lunch, first to choose playground equipment, and extra recess time. The "blue-eyes" were to sit at the front of the classroom, and the "brown-eyes" in the rear. The "blue-eyes" were encouraged to play separately from the "brown-eyes" and Elliott went as far as to establish separate water fountains. She was quick to address the "brown-eyes" when they deviated from class rules or made other simple mistakes. She was just as quick to point out the superior behavior of the "blue-eyes" and contrasted that with the "brown-eyes" negative behavior.

At first, the "brown-eyes" resisted their new status as inferior to the "blue-eyes," so the teacher added a more sinister component. She lied and told the class that low levels of melanin (brown pigment determining hair, skin, and eye color) was scientifically known to increase intelligence and learning ability. Soon after this disclosure the "brown-eyes" began to accept their lesser status. At the same time the "blue-eyes," while tolerant of the "brown-eyes," became arrogant, bossy, and otherwise unpleasant to the "brown-eyes." The blue-eyed children did better on simple tests, they completed math and reading assignments faster and with less mistakes than the "brown-eyes" who had lost confidence, become more submissive, and were beginning to perform more poorly in class. The "brown-eyes" even avoided the blue-eyed children at recess and kept to themselves.

The following week, Elliott flipped their roles and made the "brown-eyes" superior. She told the class that she had made a mistake and that the science actually showed that high levels of melanin indicated higher intelligence. She then had the "brown-eyes" place blue collars around the necks of the "blue-eyes". Now it was the brown-eyed children who were tolerant of the "blue-eyes", and while the "brown-eyes" did adopt an air of superiority and taunted the "blue-eyes" as they had been treated, Elliott noted that it was much less intense. After two days of "brown-eyes" in the superior role, Elliott ended the exercise and asked the students to reflect on the experience.

Reflections

Do you feel this was an unethical exercise? Why? Why not?

Does the use of the word "tolerant" bother you? If so, how?

How does story illustrate expectancy theory?

How does labeling "brown-eyes" and "blue-eyes" contribute to the perception of inferiority or superiority?

Do you think this exercise left an imprint on these children as they became adults?

If so, what was the imprint?

How might this experience manifest itself in adult behavior?

How might this exercise have developed greater empathy?

References

1.   Hampson, S.E., *Mechanisms by Which Childhood Personality Traits Influence Adult Well-Being.* Current Directions in Psychological Science, 2008. **17**(4): p. 264-268.

2.   Tannen, D., *Talking from 9 to 5*. Reprint. ed. 2001, London: Virago Press.

3.   Ross, L., *The Intuitive Psychologist and His Shortcomings: Distortions in the Attribution Process.* Advances in Experimental Social Psychology, 1977. **10**: p. 174.

4.   Bandura, A., *Social learning theory.* 1977, Prentice Hall: Englewood Cliffs, N.J.

5.   Vroom, V.H., *Motivation in management.* 1965, American Foundation for Management Research: New York.

6.   Peters, W., *A class divided : then and now.* 1987, Yale University Press: New Haven.

PART ONE

INTROSPECTIONS

This section consists of chapters that explore some of the more salient aspects of what it means to be social. We will be looking inward and examining what it means to be us: how we interact with others, how we communicate with others, and how symbolism – which is essential for communication – exerts tremendous influence over how we understand and ascribe meaning to events. We will look at how we come to understand our social environment and how other forces influence our perceptions. We examine personalities and the characteristics that make us unique. We explore the concept of empathy and how it plays into our behavior and endears us to others. We also look at humor, what it is, how it works, and why. Finally, we consider emotions and how we choose to present ourselves to others.

The intent of this section is to understand what it means to be bona fide, what is authentic about us. Why do we act the way we do and how do we understand the actions of others? It is a fundamental premise of this book that before we can entertain the notion of leadership, we must be grounded in a sense of ourselves. We must grasp why we are motivated to act in certain ways and that it is ok to be who we are. The important point is not that we need to dial up particular attributes or behaviors, rather, we need to be comfortable in our own skin and that begins with understanding just what that is.

CHAPTER 1

Symbolism and Communication

"We live together, we act on, and react to, one another but always and in all circumstances we are by ourselves. The martyrs go hand in hand into the arena, they are crucified alone. Embraced, the lovers desperately try to fuse their insulated ecstasies into a single self-transcendence; in vain. By its very nature every embodied spirit is doomed to suffer and enjoy in solitude. Sensations, feelings, insights, fantasies—all are private and, except through symbols and at second hand, incommunicable. We can pool information about experiences, but never the experiences themselves. From family to nation, every human group is a society of island universes."

—Aldous Huxley[1]

Communication is the very essence of a social life. All living organisms, even bacteria, manage to communicate in some fashion. But as humans we are unique in that we communicate using symbols and abstract thought. We typically view communication as a string of words in a conversation, email, or text message. We tend to overlook the significance or richness of non-verbal communication, yet when we stop to examine it, we quickly recognize its importance. A problem arises when we communicate or process communication subconsciously. We forget or don't recognize that our visceral reaction to a comment is based more on *how* something was said rather than *what* was said. Even words left unsaid communicate a message to us. In fact, as psychologist and communication theorist Paul Watzlawick stated: "One cannot not communicate."[2] Extending Watzlawick's statement, we can add *nor can we not process the communication of others.*

Consider the basic model of all communication: Sender-Message-Channel-Receiver. Originally suggested by David Berlo in 1960, the *message* consists of various symbols understood by both the *sender* and *receiver*.[3] Added later to Berlo's model are the activities of encoding and decoding the symbols used to convey the message. There are even symbols imbedded in symbols. For example, if a *sender* communicates that a storm is coming, the *receiver* first must understand the word storm which the *sender* has conveyed using sound or graphics such as letters. Either way it is a symbolic representation of a storm. But what if the *sender*'s encoding intends the word "storm" to mean trouble? In this context, the use of the word storm has symbolic meaning beyond its negotiated, or mutually understood, face meaning. But what if the *receiver* does not decode this meaning? Or what if the *receiver* decodes this to be the meaning and it was not the intended meaning? Returning to the point that we "cannot not communicate," as the *sender*, any attempt to not send a message, constitutes a message. A *sender* intending to not communicate with a *receiver* still sends a *message*, and that message is that the *sender* does not wish to communicate.

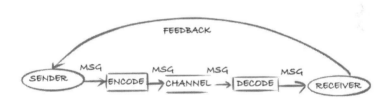

Figure 4: Berlo's Model of Communication

If we consider all of the variations of symbolism that we use in communication, we are faced with a picture of social complexity that boggles the mind. In fact, it is more than we can effectively process cognitively, so the symbols become negotiated meanings that are used as shortcuts in the communication process. These negotiated meanings can be shared by a few or by many. They are shortcuts in communication because as a result of their shared understanding, their meaning has been previously learned, and their use invokes that understanding.

Herbert A. Simon, an exceptional and very influential American political scientist, sociologist, and psychologist, is perhaps most noted for his contributions to the fields of artificial intelligence and industrial organization. One of Simon's most noted contributions to social science was the notion that people, regardless of their rational intentions, did not always conform to "rational" decision processes.[4] He suggested that as we attempt to make rational choices, we are limited by our ability to cognitively process all of the requisite information to achieve a true rational decision. He called this "bounded rationality."

He suggested that as humans faced with limited cognitive resources, we *satisfice,* or get to a just good enough solution. This means that we must take certain cognitive shortcuts to arrive at an adequate decision, because a perfect decision would require us to process information in an infinite loop. The result would be a constant stream of new incoming information to add to the existing information as we try to achieve a perfect solution. So, as we process information, we stop gathering new information at some point on that curve. This *satisfice point* is where we make the determination that we have enough information to make our decision. It is the breakeven point beyond which the time that would be spent gathering more information is more valuable if spent elsewhere on some other decision.

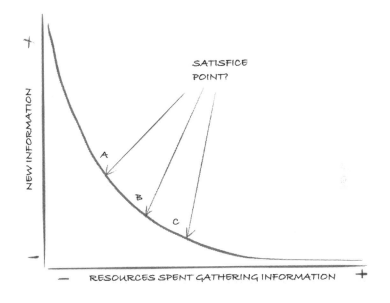

Fig

ure 5: Satisficing

The question then becomes, "at what point am I willing to satisfice and at what potential cost?" Obviously on issues of great importance we gather more information in an attempt to remove more uncertainty, and on lesser issues, we can get to a decision quickly. Of course, there are innumerable sources of information, each must be sourced, validated, weighted, sorted, stored, and placed in context with other information; and of course, the more information that is available, the more time it takes to process.

As we satisfice, symbols become a part of our shortcut process because they hold previously investigated understanding, including deeply imbedded and subconscious meanings. The use of symbols allows us to speed-up our information processing, make a determination, and then move on to the next one. We do this countless times every day. If we did not, if we pursued perfect information, we would never get past our first investigation.

With symbols, as useful as they are, they are still proxies or representations of something. They are saddled with idiosyncratic assignments of meaning and we harbor a multitude of these subconscious meanings. They are mostly learned through our life experiences, and we tend to not pause to examine them when they are invoked. For example, symbols representing authority, such as a policeman's uniform, the white lab coat of a scientist, or even the suit and tie of a businessman, all invoke meaning largely outside of our conscious thought. In fact, thinking symbolically is the foundation of everything we do – it is the very essence of our social existence.

We are bombarded and inundated with symbolic meaning, from how we dress, to physical symbols and artifacts, to communication styles, and even ceremonies and rituals. While all of these symbols and their associated meanings are used to "satisfice" in our thinking, they also can constrain or detour our thinking in ways that we may not be aware. Consider the experiment conducted by Stanley Milgram in the 1960s at Yale University. In this experiment Milgram showed that participants chosen at random would deliver seemingly lethal shocks to other people when directed by an authority figure.[5] The symbolic meaning of a white lab coat and clipboard conveyed authority and resulted in average people shortcutting their decision-making process in deference to that authority. Milgram showed that the simple symbolic representation of an authority figure caused the subjects to satisfice and defer responsibility for their actions to the "expert." While largely criticized as unethical, Milgram was able to demonstrate the frailty of human decision processes and explain how abhorrent human actions such as the Nazi behavior in the Holocaust can occur.

In a similarly criticized study, but one in which perhaps more symbolism was invoked, Philip Zimbardo conducted the Stanford prison experiment where he randomly assigned the role of prison guard or prisoner to college students who had volunteered to participate. In this experiment, captured in the documentary *Quiet Rage*, Zimbardo made heavy use of symbolism by dressing the guards in uniforms and the prisoners in smocks, and establishing a mock prison with cells and holding areas.[6] The planned two-week study was ended early due to the real emotional trauma felt by the prisoners and the guards. Steeped in symbolism, both guards and prisoners quickly assumed the roles of their real-life counterparts and actually became "guards" and "prisoners" in their own minds.

Social interactions in organizations are steeped in symbolism. From the big desk in the corner office, to staff meetings, to the conversation at the water-cooler, organizations are communicating to their members what is valued. In their widely influential book on organizational leadership, *Reframing Organizations*, Lee Bolman and Terrence Deal suggested there are four frames from which leaders can orient their observations and make assessments about organizational needs and institutional challenges, and address them with appropriate actions.[7] Ideally, these four frames (Structural, Human Resource, Political, and Symbolic) are used in concert and in varying degrees when implementing a change effort. Focusing on just the symbolic perspective, there is much to be learned from organizational culture. Among other points, they proposed that "in the face of uncertainty and ambiguity people create symbols to resolve confusion, increase predictability, provide direction, and anchor hope and faith." In other words, we use symbols as an antidote to the anxiety caused by the unknown.

So, if our rational thinking is undercut by symbolic meaning, how do we know what we know? How do we come to understand and negotiate the meaning of our symbols? Charles Peirce, in his essay "The Fixation of Belief," suggested that what we know or deem to be true is based on four fundamental methods: *Tenacity, Authority, Reason,* and *Science.*[8]

The first, *tenacity,* is a truth that is known to the individual or group. There is no questioning or testing of the truth, it is simply something we hold as true. It is true because it has always been true. It was true for my parents and their parents, so it is true for me. *I can't book a flight next Friday, it's the 13th.* This truth is not based on a specific line of reasoning, instead it tends to be generalized and based on a lack of understanding causality. It often is manifest as fate, magic, luck, prophecy, superstition, or a belief that certain outcomes are the result of unrelated prior events or forces.

Next, the *authority* method is a truth that is established through a trusted or credible source. We know something to be true because we trust the source of the information. As previously discussed, this can also be heavily influenced by symbolism in that our experts are themselves symbols of knowledge. *My doctor said my condition will require surgery to correct.* The authority truth is the tendency to attribute (usually greater than justifiable) truth to the opinion of an authority figure.

The third method of knowing, *reason,* is the method of experience and proper exercise of cognition, Far superior to tenacity and authority, but not systematic, this is how we come to understand an event or social exchange. We may know or feel we know something through personal experience. This is often a powerful approach for many people and is highly influenced by symbolism and context. *I am not comfortable sharing my home address with that salesperson.* The reason method of knowing invokes the power of comprehension, inference making, sense-making, and rational examination of cause and effect.

The *science* method, the final and superior way of knowing, leverages process or systems for defining what is true. The process produces results, is verifiable by others, and is self-correcting. At its core, the scientific method is systematic observation, measurement, and experimentation which results in the formulation, testing, and modification of hypotheses about the presumed relations among natural phenomena. *I know that cigarette smoking is bad for you because countless studies have shown harmful effects to the heart and lungs.* The science method of truth reveres the process over the outcome and that process involves inductive thinking, careful observation, rigorous skepticism, and the testing and refinement of hypotheses.

Each of these ways of knowing is imperfect. Our *tenacity* truth may be based on our social indoctrination or cultural socialization. Our *authority* truth may be from a source that we think is credible, but they are in error, or our attribution that they are an expert is flawed. Our *reason* truth may be limited or constrained by our life experiences and skewed by the attributions we make. And our *scientific* truth may be based upon flawed assumptions, data, or analysis. In other words, they are all subject to our "satisficing."

A bona fide leader is first and foremost a communicator. They understand the value of encoding messages when communicating. They understand the importance of the clarity of the message and the power of symbolism used in communication. Bona fide leaders understand that symbols assist us in satisficing and are important in communications. Finally, an authentic leader prioritizes rigor in validating truth by essentially starting with the scientific approach, then reason, then authority, and finally tenacity, if necessary.

On Knowing

"Fifteen hundred years ago everybody 'knew' the Earth was the center of the universe. Five hundred years ago, everybody 'knew' the Earth was flat, and fifteen minutes ago, you 'knew' that humans were alone on this planet. Imagine what you'll 'know' tomorrow."
—K talking to Edwards in *Men in Black*

Reflections

Do you believe in something that is not widely believed in?

Have you ever been ostracized, ridiculed, or persecuted for what you believe?

What do you know to be true?

What method leads you to this conclusion?

What has made you redefine what you know in the past?

How do you deal with surprises?

Has a surprise ever led you to a new "know?"

References

1. Huxley, A., *The Doors of Perception*. 1954, New York: Harper.

2. Watzlawick, P., et al., *Pragmatics of human communication; : a study of interactional patterns, pathologies, and paradoxes*. 1967, Norton: New York.

3. Berlo, D.K., *The process of communication; an introduction to theory and practice*. 1960, Holt, Rinehart and Winston: New York.

4. Simon, H.A., *Administrative behavior*. 4. ed. ed. 1997, New York u.a: Free Press.

5. Milgram, S., *Behavioral Study of obedience*. The Journal of Abnormal and Social Psychology, 1963(4): p. 371.

6. Musen, K. and P.G. Zimbardo, *Quiet Rage The Stanford Prison Experiment*. 2004, Philip G. Zimbardo and Stanford University: Stanford, CA.

7. Bolman, L.G. and T.E. Deal, *Reframing organizations*. 5. ed. ed. 2013, San Francisco, Calif: Jossey-Bass.

8. Peirce, C.S., *Essays in the philosophy of science*. 1957, Liberal Arts Press: New York.

CHAPTER 2

Making Sense and Learning

"Sense: Perception through the intellect; apprehension; recognition; understanding; discernment; appreciation."

—Merriam-Webster[1]

"So we live exclusively in relation to others, and what disappears from our lives is solitude. Technology is taking away our privacy and our concentration, but it is also taking away our ability to be alone."

—William Deresiewicz[2]

Every interaction we have with others, every conversation, every exchange, and every non-verbal signal needs to be interpreted and processed in our minds and acted upon or dismissed. In what amounts to an onslaught of stimuli, we navigate our way through, satisficing and constantly processing, responding or dismissing without much conscious thought.

In today's world of connectivity, this flow of stimuli has only intensified. We are in a near-constant social environment, and therefore are processing, responding, or dismissing virtually all the time. True solitude has become an increasingly difficult state to achieve. Perhaps the only time we are not engaged in social activity is when we are sleeping. However, even then, our phones are only a few inches and decibels away from social connectivity, and in our subconscious minds we are likely even dreaming about a social encounter.

What does this mean for us? Could it be that this constant state of processing and responding denies us the ability to make sense of our social environment accurately? And if so, do we find ourselves in a near-constant state of frustration? For most of us, the lack of solitude and deep reflection in our lives has resulted in a lack of rigor in how we make sense. We rely on symbols, biases, attitudes, past experiences, and other people to help us as we process and respond, day in day out, without recognizing we are engaged in a process of making sense of our social surroundings. What does it mean to make sense? What is sense? And if we know what sense is, how do we make it?

Merriam-Webster defines sense as: *"Perception through the intellect; apprehension; recognition; understanding; discernment. Appreciation."*[1] Using this definition, it can be inferred that "sense" is the understanding of something that has been perceived. In other words, when we make sense of something, we are looking back at an occurrence and assigning meaning or understanding to it. Sense is our understanding of the world around us. It is the meaning we ascribe to every event, interaction, or observation. As learners, we perceive, interpret, and categorize these stimuli based on our schema or mental map. Once classified, we choose a "sense" from a pool of "senses" we have previously and subconsciously banked in our mind, and then we respond. All of this happens in the blink of an eye and happens nearly continuously.

New sense or learning occurs when we are surprised or faced with something we did not expect. This surprise stops our subconscious processing and invokes a more conscious one. According to Leon Festinger, we have to reconcile the surprise and seek consistency between beliefs and opinions.[3] Essentially, it is *cognitive dissonance* that we must process and categorize so we can reconcile it from what we expected. This is the power of difference. Looking back at Bandura's triad of *reciprocal determinism,* it is the difference between *self, action,* or *others.*[4] This difference stands out. It makes us think about it. It challenges our existing mental frameworks and attitudes, and may even foster the invention of new ones. To understand the power of difference, let's look at how we make sense and how the process of making sense often creates a paradox, since how we make sense can influence the sense we make.

In his book *Sensemaking in Organizations*, Karl Weick proposed four different levels of subjectivity when making sense: *intra-subjective, inter-subjective, generic-subjective*, and *extra-subjective*.[5] At each level above the first level, our sense is increasingly shaped by social influences. Weick also argued that making sense is, by nature, a retrospective activity. In other words, we cannot make sense of something until we have experienced or perceived it. This is a critical point because it illuminates the most important aspect of making sense. It calls upon us to scrutinize how we understand what we just experienced or witnessed. What are the emotions we feel, or we perceive others to feel? What tools do we use to make sense of each interaction or observation? What are our past experiences? What are the attitudes and opinions of others? What are our values and beliefs? What we "see" is as much a product of "who we are" as it is a product of "what is." All our life experiences and previous senses are invoked with each new learning event.

As noted above, Weick suggested we have four levels of making sense. The nested nature of these levels implies that while they are each distinct, their form of subjectivity can influence sense-making simultaneously. He called the most basic level the *intra-subjective sense*. Although each time we must make sense of what we perceive we are making a unique product of our own creation. Yet the making of sense is still largely a social endeavor and it is heavily influenced by others. Even when we make sense of things without the physical presence of others, our perceptions of their opinions and attitudes influence what we think. That said, we still invoke subjectivity in solitude differently than we do in the presence of others. Not only do we make sense differently, but we also make a different sense. When making sense in solitude, we are alone in our perceptions; we make new sense based on our experiences and past sense. At this level of making sense, we are more vulnerable to our fears and biases than we would be in the presence of another. This begs the question: how can we learn new sense when our current sense processes all sense? The answer to this is the very essence of why an appreciation of how we make sense and how we learn is a critical prelude to any discussion on social influence. Consider the Aldous Huxley quote from the previous chapter:

> *Even though we make sense in solitude, it is not true solitude because as previously mentioned, we still feel the influence of others even if they are not present. But consider how this process of making sense changes when we get to make the sense with another.*[6]

The process of making sense now turns into a collaboration. This *inter-subjective sense*, as Weick called it, is made when we actively engage another to make sense of some event – now we are negotiating the very meaning of what occurred. In this shared subjectivity, we share perceptions of what occurred, and while there may be differences in those perceptions, those differing perceptions present to us a surprise or "difference" that must be resolved. They cause us to reconsider and even question our own perceptions. *Perhaps my perception is wrong. Maybe I need to think about this again.* Not only are we negotiating what we perceived, but we are also negotiating what it means. Me: *I think the boss is angry.* Co-worker: *No, the boss isn't angry, she just met with a difficult client and is frustrated.* That input from a co-worker has just introduced a "difference" from the reality or the sense that I had made in solitude. Now I see the expression on the boss's face in a completely different light. It went from being a potentially hostile situation for me to one of empathy for my boss. Yet the only aspect of my sense that changed was that I considered the "sense" of my co-worker.

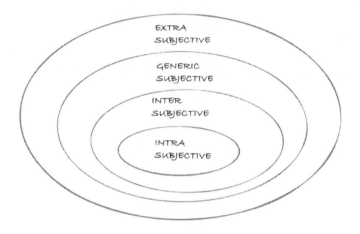

ure 6: Weick's Levels of Sensemaking

At yet a higher level of social integration, Weick suggested, was the *generic-subjective sense*. At this level sense we become heavily influenced by our role-sets. Role-sets are those roles we find ourselves in (teacher, student, team member, family member) that place expectations upon our behavior. These expectations are in the form of proscriptions and prescriptions for our behavior and perhaps even our sensemaking. This level of sensemaking subjectivity relinquishes some degree of intra-subjective sense to conform to the subjectivity shared by the group, and allows for individuals to be *interchanged* with very little impact on the patterns of interaction. Think of the inter-changeability of groups or teams you are a member of. In a strongly coupled or close-knit group, the absence of one of the members does not make a significant impact on the group itself. Consider the "sense" of a high performing sports team or the U.S. Marines.

Finally, the *extra-subjective sense* is almost a perceived sense because it is how cultural influence impacts our thinking. While we are unilateral participants in intra-subjective sense, partners in inter-subjective sense, and contributors to generic-subjective sense, we are passive receivers of extra-subjective sense. Subjectivity at this level is our perception of what is widely or generally understood by society, industries, organizations, or other large social entities. The result is an implicit or generally regarded "sense" such national culture or patriotism. Ideals such as individualism, collectivism, respect for authority, justice, patriotism, etc., where a shared set of values or shared meaning serve as "sense" guideposts when we are making our individual sense. In essence it is an abstraction of ideals derived from interactions with others.

At its basic meaning, our making of sense is about structuring of the unknown or restructuring what was known. Recall that what we "know" is based on one of the four methods as presented by Peirce. What occurs when a higher method of knowing refutes what is "known" through a lesser method? Is this a surprise? The Merriam-Webster dictionary defines surprise as "the feeling caused by something unexpected or unusual." Is it unexpected or unusual because it goes against what we think we know? So when this surprise occurs, how do we reconcile the contradiction in what we think we know? We make sense of it.

Sense-making is more than merely the placement of stimuli into a mental framework (thereby subjecting it to our biases and satisficing); instead, and as Weick put it, it is the "reciprocal interaction of information seeking, meaning ascription, and associated responses."[5] It is important to note that the making of sense differs from interpretation (which is a form of explanation, not creation). Interpretation merely results in an acceptable and approximate translation or a satisficing. Making of new sense is about authoring as well as interpretation, it is about creation as well as discovery, it is about the *how* we interpret, it is about an activity or process rather than a product, and it is less about discovery than it is about understanding why the discovery is important to us.

So why do we care about making sense? It is critical to understanding who we are. It illuminates for us the mental frames that dictate our very understanding of the world around us. It is also important because as we come to understand our own sense-making, we then make sense at a higher level of cognitive engagement. The power of the sense created can have a dramatic impact on the behavior of individuals, groups, and even societies. Consider the Holocaust. The *extra-subjective sense* of the Nazis was fundamentally flawed, yet it was a shared sense that allowed for abhorrent treatment of others to be viewed as necessary by an entire population. Another example is the Abu Gharib incident, where soldiers guarding enemy prisoners grossly mistreated them. A failure of the *generic-subjective sense,* allowed for the inhumane treatment of prisoners to somehow seem justified and normal (also consider Jim Jones, the Charles Manson family, etc.).

Finally, consider the failure at the *inter-subjective sense*. Think of every situation you have been in where you did something you regret. How many times was your regrettable behavior influenced by the presence of another? How many times have you observed that *whenever so and so are together…*? Sometimes the sense we make together with another is very different than we would make by ourselves or with yet someone else. What is most interesting is that failure of sense-making at a higher level of subjectivity tends to cascade down to a flawed sense at a lower level of subjectivity. This nested nature of the levels of sensemaking suggests that our sense is a complex composite of influences and is less about what we think and more about what others think.

So then, how do we retain the sense that we make? This is what we mean when we refer to learning. As we constantly negotiate new "sense," we accumulate our self-constructed knowledge of the world and the people around us. Interestingly, we often seem to have a clearer understanding of everyone else more so than we do of ourselves.

Researchers interested in how social learning occurs typically point to two basic categories of knowledge: explicit and tacit.[7] The first, *explicit knowledge,* is that knowledge that retains facts and theories. This type of knowledge can be written down and shared with others across time and space. The second category, *tacit knowledge,* is only discernable through its application. It represents the "unwritten." Much of social exchange is in this category. It is nuanced by subtle non-verbal signals and innuendos. Furthermore, and in contrast to explicit knowledge, tacit knowledge is difficult to articulate and therefore slow and costly to communicate.

In regards to social learning however, combining explicit and tacit knowledge with an emphasis on social connectivity and interaction creates yet another type of knowledge: *social knowledge*. This type of knowledge is more than the aggregation of group members' knowledge, it also the product of the various relationships and connections within that group. This knowledge is based on the accumulated experiences of individuals which gets embedded in the groups to which they belong and is passed onto other members in that group.[8]

Sensemaking is a critical activity in leadership. As leaders make sense of the environment or context, they are often ascribing meaning for others. As leaders formulate their own intra-subjective sense, they invariably influence the sensemaking of others at the extra-subjective, generic-subjective, and inter-subjective levels, perhaps even simultaneously. A bona fide leader is very aware of the sense they make, and subsequently how to best communicate to those that follow. Sensemaking is critical to leading and, at its core, the role of a leader is to shape the sense of others.

The following short story provides an example of the levels of sensemaking and types of knowledge as a young man enters into the uncertain experience of military basic training. After reading the story, take a moment to reflect on the questions that follow.

Boot Camp

The young man was headed to boot camp. He felt others size him up as he walked by them in the airport. He was sizing them up as well. What did they think of him? Could they sense his dread? His fear? His shoulders slouched as he stood at the gate waiting to board his plane. He felt so alone. He was a nameless, faceless young man in an endless sea of people.

As he boarded the plane, he wondered if he was making a big mistake. He knew that there was no going back, because he had already taken the oath.

While on the plane, his thoughts were running wild. He has heard all of the stories. He knew that the friendliness of the flight attendants was perhaps the last friendliness he would experience for a while. When he arrived at the airport he was greeted by a young lady in uniform. She was stoic but not mean. She was helpful but not friendly. She directed him to the bus that would take him to boot camp. At this point the young man's heart was racing. He has heard all of the stories and watched the movies. *This is where it all begins*, he thought.

Perhaps this was a mistake. His old job was not that bad after all. He wondered if he'd be able to handle the pressure. What if he couldn't? He'd be sent home humiliated. He knew that he must survive boot camp, he had no other choice. He wondered what his drill sergeant would be like. *Maybe things have changed and they're like the uniformed lady in the airport – not mean, just not friendly*. He thought of all those soldiers who had done this before him – millions, he was certain. He remembered the knot he would get in his stomach when his father would yell at him. He wondered if his drill instructor would cause that same feeling. He worried about having no privacy. *Do they still sleep in small cots in a big room? What about bathroom breaks? Showers?*

All of these thoughts were racing through his mind as he tried to make sense of what he was feeling. The only sense he could make at this point is what had already occurred. The trip to the airport, the ride on the airplane, the arrival at the airport, the young lady in uniform, and now sitting on the bus with twenty other young men and women. Each of those individuals were also deep in their own private thoughts. They were all making their own sense in solitude and speculating about what would happen next.

The bus pulled up to a building with a lot of uniformed men and women standing around talking. *Perhaps this is it. Maybe they don't do it like they used to*, the young man mused. As the bus stopped, one of the men from the group walked toward the bus and turned to the group he was talking with and made some comment. They all laughed. Witnessing this, the young man thought to himself, *OK, this isn't going to be so bad after all.* As the uniformed man approached the bus, the bus driver, who had not uttered a word, opened the door and the uniformed man stepped up into the bus.

The silence in the bus was shattered with an eruption of rage. The uniformed man that stepped onto the bus was now shouting at the top of his lungs. For some reason the young recruit felt that feeling he used to get when his father would yell at him. The recruit was instantly confused. *Why is he so mad? What have we done? What does he want us to do?* He thought to himself that the drill instructor was the fiercest looking man he had ever seen, the look in his eyes were those of absolute loathing and rage. *This guy could kill me.* He heard someone shout something about getting off the bus, so the young recruit jumped out of his seat along with all of the other recruits. The line to get off the bus was obviously not moving fast enough for the drill sergeant and his yelling was reaching that of a pitched rage. He said something like, "You are the worst bunch of recruits I have seen in a long time."

As the young recruit exited the bus, the other uniformed men and women that were mulling about were now all in a furious frenzy. Everyone was yelling. No one from the bus seemed to do anything right. The recruit just wanted to make the yelling drill sergeants happy so that they would stop screaming. He was sick to his stomach. That knot was there. He felt so alone. *When is this going to end?* he thought. *They really do hate me. I can see it in their eyes. They think I am worthless and stupid... am I?*

The group of new recruits had to endure several hours of lectures on "procedures and standards." Underwear, socks, and t-shirts folded to precise measurements and placed in a precise location in the steel locker, serial numbers recorded on every dollar carried in one's wallet, fire drill procedures, wake up times and lights out, rules for dining hall, dormitory cleanliness standards, how to make a bed, how to wear the uniform, how to address a drill instructor, etc., etc.

Several hours later and after midnight, the young recruit had just finished shoving down his first meal in hours. While he was eating, he and the others were constantly being yelled at, so needless to say, as hungry as they were, there was no enjoying the meal. He was now in his barracks with the other 50 young recruits that will be his comrades in boot camp. He has been assigned his bunk and it was time for lights out. *Finally*, he thought to himself. As he lay there mulling over the whirlwind of events over the last few hours, the recruit in the bunk next to him said, "Hey did you notice how our drill instructor's face was all sweaty and shining?"

"Yeah he must have been pretty pissed at us."

"No man, that was just an act. They all do that. When he was yelling at me after we got off the bus, I was cracking up inside because all I could think of was how many pillows he must ruin due to his oily face."

The first recruit nearly laughed out loud. "What a hilarious thought." Suddenly the demonic drill instructor was humanized. The two recruits shared some more humorous anecdotes about their drill instructor and decided they would refer to the sweaty faced ass-chewing sergeant as "Sweatin' Wesson."

The young recruit noticed how quickly the "Wesson" theme caught on. Within a couple of days, nearly every one of his fellow recruits were referring to their drill instructor as "Wesson." They continuously amused themselves with their creative derivations on the "Wesson" theme. They told stories at night while lying in their bunks.

"Old 'Slick' was in rare form today. I thought he was going to rupture a hydraulic line in his neck while he was chewing out Johnson."

"Yeah, he must have not had his Crisco for breakfast, because he was pissed off."

The recruits began to look forward to "lights out" because they would nearly always end up talking about "Wesson."

"Hey do you think he washes his face with bacon in the morning?" someone shouted.
A reply came from across the darkened room, "Naw, but I am pretty sure he drinks his coffee with two tablespoons of butter."

The entire group would burst into laughter as they did nearly every night. They all shared a common antagonist: the drill sergeant. The young recruit felt as though he could endure anything the drill instructor dished out as long as he could laugh about it at night with his fellow recruits.

Following graduation from basic training, the soldier was leaving through the same airport he had arrived at. He was in his dress uniform and could feel others' eyes upon him as he walked by. They knew what he had been through. He represented every veteran who had ever donned the uniform. He felt as though he belonged to something bigger than himself. As he stood erectly at the gate waiting to board his airplane, he was aware of the image he was projecting, he was now a soldier. He could also see in the eyes of a young woman just arriving from somewhere, and that she was heading to the same place he had just graduated from. He wanted to tell her it would all be OK, but he realized it wouldn't have changed his perspective had someone said it to him, and he thought, *Some things you just have to experience to understand.*

Reflections

Which part of the story best illustrates intra-subjective sense?

Which part of the story best illustrates inter-subjective sense?

Which part of the story best illustrates extra-subjective sense?

Which part of the story best illustrates generic-subjective sense?

How was explicit knowledge illustrated?

How was tacit knowledge illustrated?

Did relational knowledge develop?

What is the relationship of humor with sensemaking?

Are all levels of sensemaking necessary for relational knowledge to develop?

References

1. *Merriam-Webster Dictionary.* [cited 2019 Web Page]; Available from: https://www.merriam-webster.com/.
2. Deresiewicz, W., *The End of Solitude.* Chronicle of Higher Education, 2009. **55**(21): p. B.6.
3. Nelson, H.E., *A cross-cultural evaluation of Festinger's theory of cognitive dissonance.* Proceedings., 1963. **31**(1): p. 13-17.
4. Bandura, A., *Social learning theory.* 1977, Prentice Hall: Englewood Cliffs, N.J.
5. Weick, K.E., *Sensemaking in organizations.* 3. print. ed. 1996, Thousand Oaks, Calif. [u.a.]: Sage.
6. Huxley, A., *The Doors of Perception.* 1954, New York: Harper.
7. Smith, E.A., *The Role of Tacit and Explicit Knowledge in the Workplace.* Journal of Knowledge Management
2001. **5**
(4
): p. 311-321.
8. Chatterjee, S., *A Primer on Social Knowledge.* IUP Journal of Knowledge Management, 2018. **16**(4): p. 51-78.

CHAPTER 3

Personality

"Our conduct is not only rooted in first natures, it is also routed through the second natures we derive from transactions with our social ecology."

—Brian R. Little[1]

"Always be yourself, express yourself, have faith in yourself, do not go out and look for a successful personality and duplicate it."

–Bruce Lee[2]

We use the term *personality* all the time to describe the behavior of others, and others use it to describe us. We use tags such as "outgoing" or "shy," "fun-loving" or "boring." We label our friends' and acquaintances with one-word descriptors that we use to convey to others what kind of person they are. Not surprisingly, personality is one of the most actively researched topics in psychology.

As a starting point to the conversation on personality, it is important that we first distinguish between a *trait* and a *state*. A trait is a relatively static and enduring individual characteristic. Traits are what we are referring to when we describe the general characteristics of another person. Traits tend to be stable – less of a reaction and more a way of being. We are typically referring to a trait when we describe someone's general disposition. For example, when we describe one friend to another and say she is "outgoing and friendly," we are referring to her traits. Traits therefore, are generally stable across contexts. Think of someone you know that is always complaining regardless of the situation, or someone who is perpetually positive.

A state, on the other hand, is a temporary emotional condition that we find ourselves in. We are typically referring to a state when we describe a reaction to an event or some stimuli. For example, I might be described as angry, depressed, or nervous, but with each of these it would likely be noted as to why, e.g., "He is angry because his car was not repaired when it was promised by the mechanic." We can often empathize with states because we have likely experienced something similar and can recall our own state at the time.

The distinction between the two can become confusing when a trait starts to seem like a state, and vice versa. That friend who has the personality trait of "outgoing and friendly" might actually be shy at first around other women, but not men. Again, the primary way to distinguish the two is to examine how it is used. If the words "because," "due to" or some other similar conjunction are present in the sentence describing the behavior of a person, it is likely describing a state, and therefore contingent on situational dynamics. If that behavior surfaces frequently and across a wide range of situations, it may be actually be a state, and be central to their personality. Indeed, our personalities are enduring personal characteristics that comprise the characteristic patterns of how we think, feel and behave.

Psychologist Brian Little suggested that our personality has three layers: the *biogenic*, the *idogenic*, and the *sociogenic*.[1] Little described the first layer, the biogenic, as being the result of our genetics or biology. This would be the "nature" contribution to our personalities. The second layer, the idogenic, consists of those aspects of your personality that are really important to you, and therefore represent personal desires that inform your behavior. Finally, the sociogenic layer is the result of those signals you want to send the world about who you are. Little suggested that these three layers are not always in harmony with one another; and they may even be in conflict. A biogenic tendency to be assertive and stand out from the crowd may conflict with a sociogenic need to be modest. We could argue that this is the psychological labor of adulthood, a time in our life where we strive to align our sociogenic, idogenic, and biogenic natures.

Largely, researchers studying personality characteristics have agreed that personality can be grouped into five categories of characteristics.[3] Known as the "Big Five," or "Five-Factor Model," the characteristics are commonly referred to using the acronym OCEAN; the descriptors for these categories of characteristics are *Openness to new experience, Conscientiousness, Extraversion, Agreeableness*, and *Neuroticism*. This taxonomy of characteristics is generally considered to represent the basic structure of personality. Each of the individual traits encompasses a broad category of behaviors or descriptors that contains a cluster of more specific ones called *facets*.[4]

Openness to new experience represents the degree to which a person has an adaptive capacity or is curious versus being highly structured or risk-averse. Openness reflects a certain intellectual curiosity, a creative nature, and a preference for variety and novelty. It is also points to an active imagination, and a desire for independence. Someone with a high level of openness could also be interpreted as being unpredictable or scattered, while someone with low openness may appear to be driven by routine, determined, practical, logical, and perhaps even dogmatic.

Conscientiousness refers to a tendency to be organized and dependable, aiming for achievement, and having a preference for planning over spontaneity. A person with high conscientiousness would be described as focused, purposeful and on-task, whereas a low conscientiousness score would reflect more of a laissez-faire, easy-going, and carefree spirit. High conscientiousness can also be perceived as strong-willed, stubborn, and even obsessive; conversely, a person with low conscientiousness is often described as being flexible and spontaneous, but can also be perceived as disorganized and unreliable.

The high energy characterization that is associated with *extraversion* also includes perceptions of positive emotions, assertiveness, social skill, and a gregarious nature. People with a high extraversion score are generally viewed as being very outgoing and possessing high social energy while those on the lower side tend to be more solitary and reserved.

Extraversion is often perceived as seeking "center-stage," and even being pushy, while those with low extraversion are perceived as reserved, pensive, or even aloof, standoffish, or self-absorbed.

Those high in *agreeableness* are viewed as friendly, socially astute, sincere and empathetic as opposed to challenging, selfish, and insincere. They tend to be considerate of others and more cooperative rather than self-focused and antagonistic. It also reveals a tendency to trust more quickly and a desire to be helpful to others. Those with high agreeableness are often seen as simple, naïve, and even submissive, while those low in agreeableness are often considered to be highly competitive or even argumentative and untrustworthy.

The final dimension, *neuroticism* is different from the other four in that a high score has no positive attributes associated with it. A high neuroticism score would be indicative of someone who is thin-skinned and generally of a nervous nature. This dimension is manifest in the tendency to express dour emotions such as anger, anxiety, or sadness, frequently or easily. Neuroticism tends to be perceived as a lack of emotional stability and a low ability to control impulses. A person with high neuroticism projects a low need for stability and emotes in a reactive and excitable manner. A person high on neuroticism can be seen as very dynamic, but they can also be perceived as unstable or insecure. Those with a low score, on the other hand are viewed as stable and calm, but can also be seen as disinterested and uninspiring.

While the Big Five are the most cited and referenced, some psychologists feel there are other traits not covered by the Big Five, such as Machiavellianism, honesty, conservativeness, egotism, thrill-seeking, and humor, to name a few. Still, the Big Five has been the focus of countless studies seeking to use personality as a predictor of everything from academic success to leader performance.

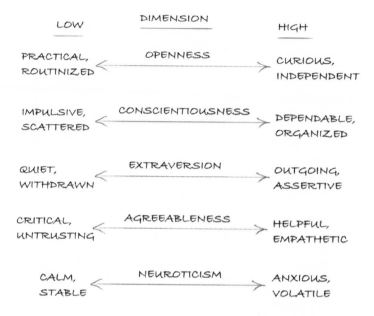

LOW	DIMENSION	HIGH
PRACTICAL, ROUTINIZED	OPENNESS	CURIOUS, INDEPENDENT
IMPULSIVE, SCATTERED	CONSCIENTIOUSNESS	DEPENDABLE, ORGANIZED
QUIET, WITHDRAWN	EXTRAVERSION	OUTGOING, ASSERTIVE
CRITICAL, UNTRUSTING	AGREEABLENESS	HELPFUL, EMPATHETIC
CALM, STABLE	NEUROTICISM	ANXIOUS, VOLATILE

Figure 7: Big Five Dimensions of Personality

For the Big Five to be descriptive, think of each characteristic on a sliding scale rather than a high-low binary. Along this sliding scale, there will be many specific attributes called *facets* that are more precise descriptors of behavior.[4] Consider that on each of these Big Five sliding scales you can plot a specific point based on a measure or score. This score would correlate with a specific facet, but more interestingly, when all five scores are plotted, there emerges a composite picture that can be arrayed in spider diagram polygon. The shape of the polygon represents the entire Big Five, or the composite personality.

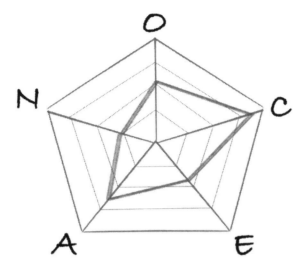

Figure 8: Personality Spider Diagram

In this spider diagram, the personality displayed is moderate on openness to new experience, high on conscientiousness, moderate on extraversion, moderately high on agreeableness, and low on neuroticism. Using facets from each personality dimension, we can describe this person (in OCEAN order) as down-to-earth, hard-working, reserved, good-natured, and even-tempered.

If we accept that our personalities are distinct and unique to us and can largely be described, and even plotted by the Big Five, where does the variability come from? Why are some of us high in some dimensions and low in others? How and when do our personalities form? According to Eric Erikson, a noted developmental psychiatrist, personality develops in a specific order through eight pre-determined stages of psychosocial development, from infancy to adulthood.[5] He argued that during each stage (he originally proposed there were eight stages ranging from birth to 65 years and older, but later added a ninth, a very old age), aspects of our personality develop or emerge as the result of "psychosocial crisis."[5, 6]

He also suggested there were basic "virtues" that emerged in each of these stages, ranging from "hope" to "wisdom." This interactional perspective suggests that our personality may actually be formed by a series of dispositional and situational collisions in predetermined developmental stages, and that our dispositions interact with the situation to determine how we progress through each successive stage. The result is a unique "unfolding" of our personalities, where the manner in which we navigate the "stages" is to some degree determined by how we navigated all of the previous stages.

So then, if we have a distinct personality developed throughout our lifespans, and that personality is the result of "collisions," what is the starting point for our dispositional traits? In other words, how much of our personality is a result of genetics? Interestingly, the line between disposition and situation is becoming more blurred. Bill Sullivan, a professor of pharmacology and microbiology, argues that our genes not only determine our physiological makeup, but they also are a major contributor to our personality and behavior. He suggests that a true self-understanding requires knowledge of how the environment can actually modify DNA through a process called *epigenetics*.[7]

Epigenetics may explain how the behavior of our parents may be passed down biologically to us. But it may also be the bridge that connects disposition and situation, as it has been used to explain the mutual interchange between the heredity and the environment. This view encompasses all of the possible factors that result in the development of our traits and how situational dynamics influence our disposition and how our disposition influences the way we respond to situations.

Followers choose to follow leaders based on many variables not least of which is their personality. How leaders react (states) to situations is observed and attributions are made. If similar behavioral reoccurrences are noted, the attribution will likely be that of a trait. If the behavior seems out of character, our sensemaking may assign a causal factor (thereby rendering it a state rather than a trait) and judge it to be either appropriate or not. Regardless, leaders are being watched all the time by others and every behavior gets ascribed a meaning. Bona fide leaders understand this and regulate their behavior accordingly. Also, bona fide leaders understand that unconvincing or inauthentic personality presentations ultimately undermine trust, and therefore they acknowledge and embrace their personality.

The Last Day of School

The five friends were often seen playing together. They were always engaged in some game or activity – hide-and-seek, kickball, racing their bicycles, football, you name it. They were fortunate to all live on the same block and while they would not have likely chosen each other as friends if they only met at school, they were virtually inseparable in their neighborhood. One of their favorite weekend adventures was to spend the day exploring the "swamps."

The swamps weren't really swamps, they were actually treeless cow pastures rimmed with ditches and low areas that pooled water. To the boys, it was a vast untamed wilderness that was home to all kinds of mysteries and wild creatures. During their excursions, they would often see muskrats, garter snakes, bull frogs, and countless other creatures that lived in this low-lying area.

On a day that was to be the last time they would all be together at the swamps, they had stopped at a favorite spot on the edge of a small gully to discuss their futures. They were in the last week of sixth grade, and while they were top of the social hierarchy in their elementary school, next year they would be at the bottom in middle school. They shared varying degrees of anxiety about this transition and it was increasingly the topic of discussion among them. This day was no different.

Clay was the most adventurous of the bunch. He was the most excited about the transition to middle school, as the daily bus ride would be a welcome departure from the routine of walking or riding their bikes to school as they had done for most of elementary school.

Darren was mostly concerned about having multiple teachers and the level of difficulty of the school work. Always the studious one, he had heard that in middle school there was homework every night and sometimes on the weekend.

Rudy, while nervous about the bigger boys and bullying, was looking forward to making new friends and perhaps meeting new girls. Middle school would be fed from the students of four different elementary schools, and the multiple class schedule would make it easy to meet new people.

Mario just wanted them all to stick together and hoped their friendship would remain intact. He loved hanging out with the other four and was concerned that new friends would infringe on their bonds.

Brad was nearly despondent about all of it. New settings made him anxious, as did being the youngest class at school, not to mention how hard the classes would be and the fact they would no longer have recess. He felt deeply saddened at the thought that this was the beginning of the end of a chapter of his childhood.

As their conversation flitted about from topic to topic, person to person, Darren chimed in that he was worried about what Mr. Burgess was going to think. Mr. Burgess was their sixth-grade teacher, and this was the last day of school.

It was Clay that just a few days before had recommended that they skip school and go to the swamps. Mario had immediately chimed in and said that it would be fun. Rudy was all in because he'd get to spend an entire day with his buddies – his favorite thing to do. Brad had been the only naysayer, as he was worried about getting caught and what his parents might impose as a punishment – he could be on restriction all summer. Darren had remarked that it wasn't like they'd be doing any schoolwork on the last day of school anyway, so it's not like it would hurt their grades.

As the morning moved to afternoon and they started to make their way out of the swamps so that they would arrive home at the usual time, Darren, looking forward to his parents' reactions to his straight-A report card, had a realization. REPORT CARDS! In their excitement to embark on their adventure, not one of them had considered this little detail. They would have to go see Mr. Burgess to get their report cards.

As the five walked in the classroom with dried mud on their shoes, pants, and shirts, and sunburnt faces, Mr. Burgess leaned on his desk holding the five report cards like a hand in a poker game. They didn't notice the twinkle in his eyes as he made each one promise to tell their parents what they did on the last day of school.

Reflections

Could you detect the personality differences in each boy?

Do you think those differences enhanced or hindered their friendships?

Is there a personality trait that you feel is dominant in this story?

Do you think that the decision to skip school was a function of their collective personalities?

Which of the boys, if removed from the "skip school" conversation would have had the most impact on the decision of the group?

Which of the boys' personalities is most like your own?

Do you recall from your own childhood a similar misadventure? If so, how might it have influenced who you are today?

References

1.   Little, B.R., *Me, Myself, and Us: The Science of Personality and the Art of Well-Being.* 2014: New York:; Perseus Books, PublicAffairs. xiv.
2.   Little, B.R., *Free Traits, Personal Projects and Idio-Tapes: Three Tiers for Personality Psychology.* Psychological Inquiry, 1996. **7**(4): p. 340.
3.   Digman, J.M., *Personality Structure: Emergence of the Five-Factor Model.* Annual Review of Psychology, 1990. **41**(1): p. 417-440.
4.   Costa Jr, P.T. and R.R. McCrae, *Domains and Facets: Hierarchical personality Assessment Using the Revised NEO Personality Inventory.* Journal of personality assessment, 1995. **64**(1): p. 21.
5.   Erikson, E.H. and J.M. Erikson, *The life cycle completed.* Extended version / with new chapters on the ninth stage of development by Joan M. Erikson. ed. 1997: W.W. Norton.
6.   Erikson, E.H., *Childhood and Society.* 1949: Norton.
7.   Sullivan, B., *Pleased to Meet Me: How Genes, Germs, and the Environment Make Us Who We Are.* 2019, Washington D.C.: National Geographic. 1-337.

CHAPTER 4

Empathy

"Outstanding coaches and mentors get inside the heads of the people they are helping. They sense how to give effective feedback. They know when to push for better performance and when to hold back. In the way in which they motivate their protégés, they demonstrate empathy in action."

—Daniel Goleman[1]

Given the variability in our personalities, perhaps the starting point in trying to know another person is to try to understand what they feel. If we can understand what they are feeling or have experienced the same feeling, we open an entire range of insights into understanding their behavior. It also provides us with a rich palette of responsive behaviors to choose from when interacting with them. Assuming I am high on the personality dimension of agreeableness, and I can empathize with your sorrow, I can likely show my understanding by emoting in a situationally appropriate way. This ability to understand others' emotional states is known as empathy. Yet empathy is more than the ability to detect what others feel, but it is extended to actually feeling it yourself.

Empathy and sympathy are very close constructs and are sometimes used interchangeably. Indeed, they are often somewhat intertwined which makes them even more difficult to differentiate. They are different however. Perhaps at the simplest level of distinction we can say that sympathy is something we show, and empathy is something we feel. That distinction implies that sympathy can be reasonably acted out, but empathy would be a much more difficult enactment. For the purposes of this discussion, we will just go with the understanding that true empathy is more like a contagion, something we passively catch, and subsequently emote, not something we calculate, intentionally capture, and subsequently perform.

There are many different definitions for empathy, but a common thread to most is the notion that empathy is the ability to understand and *share* the thoughts or feelings of another person. To understand and share these thoughts and feelings, it's not necessary to have been through the same experiences or circumstances, rather empathy is an attempt to better understand the other person by trying to understand their thoughts and feelings. Empathy is more than the ability to perceive what others feel, it is also to experience that emotion yourself.

If you can read another person's emotions then you can both avoid making social mistakes and can also better understand who they are. When people are in emotional states they tend to perform less and emote more. When you empathize with another person, there is a connection made and trust is formed. As a result, they may feel better in some way and less alone. From this perspective, empathy can be viewed as a social exchange where something is given (emotional support) and something is returned (appreciation).

Daniel Goleman and Paul Ekman, independent experts on how we read others' emotions and then respond to those emotions, suggested that there are different ways in which we engage in empathy. They suggested that we empathize *cognitively, emotionally,* and *compassionately.*[1, 2] Each of these forms of empathy differs in the degree to which we engage in others' emotions.

The first, *cognitive empathy*, is an understanding of what another person is feeling and what their thoughts might be. Also known as "perspective-taking", this type of empathy is useful in persuasion or motivating others. Cognitive empathy makes us better communicators, because it helps us relay information in a way that best reaches the other person. Cognitive empathy is when we try to mentally construct or understand another point of view but without the visceral emotional connection. With cognitive empathy, we can remain detached to such a degree that we're not compelled to take action to assist that person. Ekman suggests that those who are within psychology's "Dark Triad" of narcissists, Machiavellians, and sociopaths, actually leverage cognitive empathy to hurt others. In other words, an evil torturer needs cognitive empathy to better calibrate their cruelty.

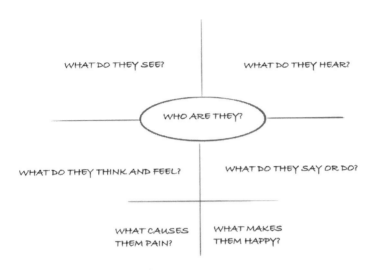

Figure 9: Empathy Map

A useful tool for developing cognitive empathy is to use an empathy map. A tool popular in business when trying to better understand customers, an empathy map poses a series of questions regarding what another person is experiencing.

What do they hear? What are their friends saying? What is their boss saying? What are others that matter to them saying?

What do they see? What are their surroundings? What does the world look like to them? Is it friendly? Is it hostile?

What do they think and feel? What are their biggest concerns? What are their priorities? What do they understand to be true? What emotions are they feeling?

What do they say or do? How do they interact with others? What is their appearance? What is their behavior?

What causes them pain? What are their fears? What are their frustrations? What causes them anxiety?

What makes them happy? What are their measures of success? What are their wants? What brings them pleasure?

Goleman and Ekman's next form of empathy, *emotional empathy,* is described as less of a calculus and more of an actual physical feeling. It is feeling what others are feeling as though their felt emotions are ours. Also known as "affective empathy," emotional empathy is when we are the most perceptive of another person's emotions and is most easily understood from the perspective of a mother truly feeling her child's pain. While this type of empathy can help you build emotional connections with others, it can also be a liability when we lack the ability to manage these externally sourced emotions, thereby leading to psychological exhaustion. Since emotional empathy has the potential to be a liability in the medical profession, professional caregivers often protect themselves from becoming emotionally drained by maintaining a sense of emotional distance from their patients.

Finally, Goleman and Ekman describe *compassionate empathy* as going beyond simply understanding others and even feeling their feelings. Instead, it actually motivates us to take action, to somehow assist and interject ourselves into the situation. With compassionate empathy we not only feel what another person is feeling, but are also motivated to help. Compassionate empathy is commonly on display directly after a disaster when people are most motivated to donate time and money to disaster victims. Ekman noted that compassionate empathy is the sense "that we're all connected."

To illustrate how these three forms of empathy work together, imagine that a friend's beloved pet has recently passed. Your natural reaction may be sympathy, a feeling of pity, or sorrow. While you do not have pets yourself, you do understand that your friend is feeling pain which may move you to express condolences or to send a note expressing your understanding. This is cognitive empathy, or imagining what the person is going through. How important was this pet in their daily life? How long had the pet been in their life? How close were they to this pet? Besides understanding the feelings of pain and loss, how will their life now be different?

Further examining this scenario from an *emotional empathy* perspective, consider that you will not only understand your friend's feelings (cognitive empathy), but somehow feel them yourself. You are grieving the loss of the pet as well. You are connecting with something in yourself that knows the feeling of the sadness and pain that comes from losing something you loved. Even though you've never had a pet, you do understand what loss feels like.

Finally, *compassionate empathy* would move you to take action. In addition to understanding (cognitive) and feeling (emotional) the pain of your friend's loss, you want to actually be a part of the remedy to the pain. You decide to interject yourself into your friend's situation and using your understanding of both your friend and the situation, you might ask your friend to go to a movie to take their mind off of their sorrow or visit them to alleviate their solitude. Consider that each of these types of empathy represent an escalating investment by the empathizing individual and, as such, are an increasing magnitude of social exchange.

While being empathetic can lead to better understanding, trust, and reciprocity, it is not necessarily a windfall of social benefits. Consider the very empathetic nurse or doctor. Being overly empathetic could prove to be a significant social strain as the medical professional *feels* the emotional state of all of their patients. Also consider the overdramatic individual that craves the attention of others. The empathetic individual would start to avoid being around the emotionally needy individual due to the constant drain. This could also be viewed as continuously withdrawing from the social exchange account and thereby creating a significant deficit – but more about that in Chapter 10.

According to Susan Miller, a veteran teacher and professor of early childhood education, we generally learn to be empathetic as children and through our own self-awareness.[3] Miller argued that we learn empathy through a series of stages and that as young children learn to express themselves and interact with other children, they are in the formative years of empathy development. Consider a group of children on the playground at school. Imagine several first-graders discussing a friend who is sad and crying. "Maybe she is sad because her Dad had to leave for a long trip" one of the children volunteers. Then another child chimes in with "I missed my dad when he went away on a trip." Another one adds "She could be scared too. It's always a little scary when Mommy or Daddy is not home." These conversations are all sensemaking events that lay the foundation for the development of empathy.

As young children become more aware of their own emotions, they begin to recognize those emotions in others, and as they do, they recall their own emotions. This serves to increase their emotional vocabulary and with this increased vocabulary comes the ability to communicate emotions with others. These discussions about emotions are the primary source of empathy development.

While most experts agree that we learn empathy as children, there is also general agreement that we can enhance our empathy as adults. A simple regimen of deep thinking and reflection, careful observation of others, practiced emotional self-awareness, and engaging with others has been shown to enhance each of the three types of empathy.

Developing cognitive empathy is about sharpening our inference-making. We do our best to consider all of the available information and deduce what others are feeling. The information we consider includes words spoken, physical movements, facial expressions, and other non-verbal messages such as posture and tone of voice. This means truly engaging with others to better understand them. Consider what you know about them, and be willing to learn more. Keep in mind that your interpretation of another person's mood, behavior, or thinking is shrouded in your prior experiences and biases.

To develop emotional empathy requires going even further. Since the goal is to actually share the feelings of the other person, it requires tapping into the inventory of real emotions that you have felt. When a person tells you about an emotional state, listen carefully to their words and descriptions. Take note of all of the non-verbal communications. Resist the urge to judge, rationalize, or categorize the person or situation. Avoid interrupting and trying to console by sharing your personal experience or proposing a solution. Instead, focus on understanding the how and why and tap into your reservoir of emotion and connect with the appropriate one.

Developing compassionate empathy is simply about determining what you can do to help. You can think to yourself "What would make me feel better?" Or "What helped me when I felt that way?" But use caution in assuming what worked for you will work for them in the same way. This is when you use your knowledge and understanding of who they are. You may share your own personal experiences or make suggestions, but avoid conveying the impression that you are delivering "the" remedy. Instead, relate it simply as compassion and a sense of understanding.

Perhaps the greatest attribute a bona fide leader can have is empathy towards those that follow. This would include empathy at a personal level in the form of understanding all of the other things in a person's life such as divorce, family illness, financial challenges, raising children, etc. It would also include an appreciation of all the workplace stressors such as long hours, complex tasks, workplace conflict, etc. Follower empathy would also include an appreciation for the "shared anxiety" of the followers. Tapping into this shared condition and truly understanding and feeling it provides a bona fide leader with the insights necessary to authentically connect with followers and communicate what needs to be done to mitigate the anxiety.

The Magnificent Toy Gun

The young boy with the fresh summer haircut was proud of the new toy his father had just bought him. He had marveled at the enormous toy gun just a few weeks ago at the department store. He didn't bother asking his father to buy it for him. He understood his family could not afford such things because he had overheard his parents discussing their financial problems late at night when he should have been sleeping.

Yet here he was, the proud new owner of the giant toy gun. It stood almost twice his size! It was the most wonderful toy he had ever owned. It contained every conceivable attachment the boy could think of: a mini rocket launcher, bayonet, hand-grenades, scope, compass, whistle, sound effects and an assortment of switches and buttons for which his imagination would supply numerous functions. It was beyond the boy's comprehension how his father knew of his desire for this magnificent toy or how he could even afford it. But he didn't have time to ponder these thoughts, for there were bands of imaginary criminals and enemy troops (not to mention an assortment of hideous monsters) waiting to do battle. Several hours and many victories later, he had temporarily rid his backyard (and exhausted his imagination) of make-believe enemies.

He was new in the neighborhood and anxious to make new friends, so he tried to stand a little taller as the two brothers, both older than him, approached from next door. The two brothers could not help but notice the magnificent toy gun, almost dwarfing the green-eyed little boy. After the usual exchange of names, ages, likes and dislikes, the boys set out on a noble crusade to rid the yard (once again) of all the threats to mankind.

The boy and his newfound friends were in the middle of a heated battle against a tribe of aboriginal head-hunters when the little boy's mother called him in for his lunch, and following his lunch, as he well knew, was his afternoon nap. He grudgingly left the battle scene, leaving behind his prized possession to secure his friendship with the two brothers. Later, as he was drifting off to sleep, he could hear the magnificent gun and the excited exclamations of the brothers as the battles continued.

After awakening from a short and restless nap the young boy hurried outside. All was quiet. The battles had ended and the brothers were gone. He looked around for his toy gun and could not see it anywhere. He checked the front porch, the back steps, he looked by the swing set, in the sand box, behind the hedges...then he spotted it way off to the side of his yard behind the base of a large oak tree – it was in pieces. He could not hold back the tears.

The hour he waited for his father to come home seemed like an eternity. He thought of the brothers and wondered why they would have done such a thing. He wondered if it was an accident or intentional. Was it his fault for trusting them so soon? What would he say to them when he next saw them? What would he say to his father who had obviously sacrificed something else in order to purchase the toy? As he waited, he dreaded the question that was sure to come as soon as his father arrived: "So, Son, how did you like playing with your new toy?" While he was waiting for his father to return from work, a feeling crept over him, one that he had never really felt before, at least not like this. He was not feeling sorry for himself and the loss of his toy, he was not feeling anger toward the brothers, nor was he fearing his dad's anger. Instead, at the young age of four, he was feeling sorrow for the sadness his father would feel.

Reflections

What range of emotions did you feel when reading this story?

Why had the boy learned empathy? Empathy for what?

What type of empathy did the boy experience?

What type of empathy are you experiencing in reading this?

What else was learned by the boy?

What might have been learned by the brothers?

How might this experience influence the boy as an adult?

What attributions did you make about the brothers?

What attributions did you make about the boy?

What attributions did you make about the father?

What happens next in this story?

References

1. Goleman, D., *Emotional intelligence*. 2005, Bantam Books: New York.
2. Ekman, P., *Emotions revealed : recognizing faces and feelings to improve communication and emotional life*. 2004, Henry Holt and Co: New York, N.Y.
3. Miller, S.A., *Emotional Development of Three- and Four-Year-Olds*. Growing up in stages. 2017, San Francisco: Gryphon House, Inc. 70 Pages.

CHAPTER 5

Humor

"I see humor as being fundamentally a social activity. We are much more likely to laugh with other people than when alone, and most humor arises in response to the behavior of other people or human-like traits in non-human animals. From an evolutionary perspective, I think humor evolved as a mechanism for enhancing group cohesion."

—Rod Martin[1]

Humor is the provocation of laughter and amusement. The term humor is derived from the ancient Greek medicinal philosophy which held that health and emotion were the result of the balance or imbalance of fluids in the human body, otherwise known as known as humors. So, to be in good humor or to be humorous was to have balance and to be happy or to make others happy. Humor is also a bit enigmatic in that it is both a visceral experience and well understood as to what it is, yet simultaneously it can be a complex construct to define and understand. Merriam-Webster dictionary defines humor as "that quality which appeals to a sense of the ludicrous or absurdly incongruous: a funny or amusing quality."[2]

According to Rod Martin, a psychologist who has studied humor extensively, the meaning of humor has evolved over time and has come to be considered a virtue along with other positive attributes like common sense, tolerance, and compromise.[3] Sigmund Freud even viewed humor as a defensive behavior, yet considered that it was distinct from joking which he considered aggressive. Many noted psychologists (Abraham Maslow, Gordon Allport, George Valliant) essentially adopted the position that a healthy personality is one that possesses a sense of humor that is a non-hostile, philosophical in nature, and in general, self-deprecating – which they also considered to be a somewhat rare combination.

For the purposes of our conversation, we will borrow from Martin's definition of humor and define it as: *a broad and multi-faceted construct that refers to multiple forms of a stimulus (jokes, cartoons, comedy), various mental processes involved in creating and understanding humor (getting the joke), and various physical responses to humor (smiling, laughter).* We will also consider that humor has both cognitive and emotional aspects, and that it can be a state (a cheerful mood, or in the moment) or a trait (an enduring sense of humor).

At a more basic level, we will define humor as some combination of a shared inference and degree of surprise. Martin calls this surprise an "incongruity" and in his book, *The Psychology of Humor*, he asserts that identifying incongruity is "minimally necessary for all humor." From this perspective, humor is a *communication* that intentionally or accidentally deviates from what the receiver expects. It is a surprise.

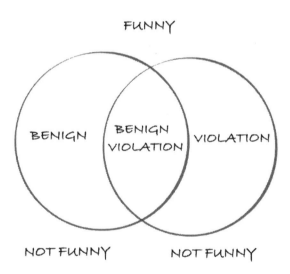

Figure 10: Benign Violation Theory

This is echoed by Peter McGraw and Joel Warner in their book *The Humor Code,* where they proposed that humor is a benign violation of expectations.[4] They use to word "violation" instead of surprise, or incongruity, but the meaning is essentially the same. Their "benign violation theory" suggests what is funny as well as what is not, and why a function of the violation is being in the middle zone of not being too benign, but also not too much of a violation. Let's consider humor from several vantage points that we have already discussed in this book. In particular, the communications model and sensemaking shed the most light on the humor construct.

From a communications model perspective, humor is created during the encoding of a message, where it is encoded in such a way as to be absurd or to provide a "surprise" to the decoder. Interestingly, for the humor to be recognized as such by the receiver of the communication, they must make the sense that the encoded surprise was intentional. This is "getting" the joke. Sometimes the intra-subjective sense does not recognize the surprise as intended humor, and it is only through inter-subjective or even generic sense that the receiver decodes the message as a humorous one.

As a part of our sensemaking processes, we make inferences. An inference is an understanding that is based on evidence and reasoning. It is an "educated guess." While we learn many things experientially, or at first hand, we also learn by making inferences based on what we already know and what we observe.

Our ability to make inference requires knowledge or experience. This implies that humor has levels of sophistication or targets of inference-making. Slapstick humor such as children's cartoons like *Road Runner* or *Tom and Jerry* are funny to children because their inference-making can create the "prediction" that results in a surprise. With more sophisticated forms of humor, such as satire, the necessary inference may be an understanding of the political landscape or of a more complex social context, such as current events. Indeed, humor can be used as a test of another's intellect and research generally supports the connection between intelligence and the ability to produce or recognize humor.

So, in the inference-making process, we create an expectation based on what we already know and what we are seeing or decoding. We have an expectation for what the message will be. With humor, we are surprised by what the message is and we must make sense of that. When in our sensemaking process we "discover" that the surprise was intended, we understand it as humor and have a visceral reaction to the discovery.

This explains why some people that we know to be humorous can make us laugh with very little communication or even only non-verbal communication. It is because we already have knowledge of their humorous communication, which results in making an inference that what they are about to communicate will be humorous. In essence, we are primed for their humor. But the best jokes are those where the surprise is complete and our sensemaking has to engage in understanding the episode.

This also explains why a joke when told the second time is not as funny as it was originally. While we can still appreciate the cleverness in the construction of the humorous communique, we are not surprised by it anymore. When we make sense of surprises, as we do when we understand humor, we are also learning. For this reason, humor can be a sophisticated form of communication in that it is manipulating another's inference-making.

The process of creating humor requires sophisticated encoding in that the communication needs to deliberately invoke sensemaking in another. In other words, humor is intentionally creating a sense of confusion, then at precisely the right moment communicating the message that reveals (through nuance or non-verbal communication) the humorous intent of the communication. This is why sarcasm often falls flat when not delivered face to face or without the benefit of priming or non-verbal communication. In a study conducted by Gil Greenhouse and Geoffrey Miller, they found that stand-up comedians have a distinctive personality profile when compared to non-comedians.[5] Among other findings, their research showed that stand-ups score higher on openness to new experience, and that this personality dimension was the only one of the Big-Five to be positively related to the ability to produce humor. Another finding was that comedians score lower on extraversion than non-comedians, suggesting that their stage personas differed from their true ones.

Now let's consider workplace humor or humor that exists within an organizational context. What makes it funny? It is that we have a shared experience base that informs our sensemaking and the inferences we draw? This is why workplace jokes would not be understood by others outside of the work context, they just would not be able to make the inference that enables them to "get" the surprise or why it is absurd. Also, from an organizational perspective, humor is often used to cope with stress.

According to the Mayo Clinic, we can experience stress relief from laughter.[6] In addition to the mental distraction from the sources of stress, they touted the short-term benefits of laughter as physiological in that it produces chemical changes in your body. They pointed out that laughter increases oxygen intake, which stimulates heart activity, lung functioning, and muscle strength; laughter also amplifies the endorphins that our brains release. Additionally, they noted that a robust laughing episode fires up and then cools down our body's response to stress, which causes a temporary increase then decrease in heart rate and blood pressure which results in a good, relaxed feeling. Finally, they point out that laughter soothes tension by increasing blood circulation and muscle relaxation, both of which work to alleviate some of the physical symptoms of stress.

Perhaps more important are the long-term effects of regular humorous episodes. The Mayo Clinic reported that it can result in an improved immune system. They noted that negative stress manifests as chemical reactions in our bodies that actually decrease the capability of our immune systems. Whereas humor and uplifting thoughts can actually release neuropeptides which help us stave off stress and potentially more serious illnesses. They suggested that our reaction to humor may actually cause the body to produce its own natural painkillers, lead to greater personal satisfaction, improvement in mood, reduction of anxiety, coping with difficult situations or trauma, and improved connecting with others.

Another potential tangible outcome of humor is the fostering of trust. Consider that for humor to be effective there must be a shared context for making inference. If someone makes us laugh, then they have predicted our sensemaking, thereby establishing a shared identity, or an *identificational trust* which will be discussed later.

Humor is an important characteristic of a bona fide leader because it is a somewhat intimate connection. To express humor or to understand someone else's attempt at humor, a bona fide leader is demonstrating connectedness. It is endearing and validates that we are encoding our messages and decoding others' properly. What we find as humorous or not humorous reveals much about our underlying traits and states as well as our knowledge and experiences.

We all find different jokes funny to different degrees, but which ones are more universally funny and why? Psychologist Richard Wiseman ran an experiment to find out.[7] In 2002 he launched a website called LaughLab where anyone around the world could submit a joke and also rate other submitted jokes. He received over 41,000 entries and about 1.5 million votes. One joke reigned supreme:

The Two Hunters

Two hunters are out in the woods when one of them collapses. He doesn't seem to be breathing and his eyes are glazed. The other guy whips out his phone and calls the emergency services. He gasps, "My friend is dead! What can I do?" The operator says "Calm down. I can help. First, let's make sure he's dead." There is a silence, then a shot is heard. Back on the phone, the guy says "OK, now what?"

Reflections

Why is this joke considered universally funny?

Did you think it was funny?

What does it mean if you did or did not?

Does the joke make you feel smarter than the hunter on the phone?

How is inference used in this joke?

What is the surprise that needs to be reconciled?

References

1. Martin, R. and A.K. Nicholas, *Three Decades Investigating Humor and Laughter: An Interview With Professor Rod Martin.* Europe's Journal of Psychology, 2016(3): p. 498.

2. *Merriam-Webster Dictionary.* [cited 2019 Web Page]; Available from: https://www.merriam-webster.com/.

3. Martin, R.A. and T.E. Ford, *The Psychology of Humor : An Integrative Approach.* Vol. Second edition. 2018, London, United Kingdom: Academic Press.

4. McGraw, P. and J. Warner, *The humor code : a global search for what makes things funny.* 2014, Simon & Schuster: New York.

5. Greengross, G. and G.F. Miller, *The Big Five personality traits of professional comedians compared to amateur comedians, comedy writers, and college students.* Personality & Individual Differences, 2009. **47**(2): p. 79-83.

6. Mayo Clinic, S., *Stress relief from laughter? It's no joke.* 2019.

7. Wiseman, R., *Quirkology : How We Discover the Big Truths in Small Things.* 2008, New York: Basic Books.

CHAPTER 6

Emotion and Self-Presentation

"Oh, what a tangled web we weave
When first we practise to deceive!"
—Sir Walter Scott [1]

When we are introspective and consider our existence as human beings, we can view ourselves as three distinct selves. The first, the *physical self,* consists of the body and all of its physical attributes. Interestingly, this "self" reveals the least about us, yet it is used most often by others to "make sense" of who we are. The second self, the *cognitive* self, consists of our consciousness, our sense of being or our awareness. This intra-subjective first-person self (i.e., me) also includes our sense of spirituality and, as discussed in the previous chapter, it is from this self that we make sense, learn, and see ourselves within the universe. Finally, we have a *presented self,* which consists of our managed projections and communications based on how we want others to perceive us.

The first self is indivisible, as it is the physical manifestation of who we are as a single biological entity. The second self is divisible at the risk of cognitive dissonance and various forms of psychosis such as schizophrenia. However, the final self, the presented self, seems to be limited only by our imagination, cognitive capacity, energy, and audiences to which we wish to perform.

The *presented self* suggests an amalgam of conjured emotions, attitudes, opinions, perspectives, actions, verbal communications, and non-verbal communications, all dialed up for effect. Every social interaction consists of a multiplicity of managed impressions directed at some audience for the purpose of influencing the audience's perception of who we are. Many social scientists have used theater as an analogy for this ubiquitous social performance. In this dramatic social production there are actors, protagonists, antagonists, heroes, villains, a stage, props, a setting, and an audience. The primary assertion here is that we are always acting to some degree. We are always playing out some part in a drama with others. This is called *self-presentation*. Some of us are better actors than others, some of us are more keenly aware of others' performances. Regardless, we are always acting to project a desired image or seeking to influence the perception of others.

Emotional Intelligence (EQ or EI) is a term used to describe our ability to understand and manage our own emotions, as well as the ability to understand and *influence* the emotions of others. As discussed in the empathy chapter, the term "emotional intelligence" was made popular by Daniel Goleman.[2] Consider the relevance of EQ to the notion of empathy and the ability to encode and decode with sophistication.

Researchers studying EQ have focused on looking at EQ as either a trait or an ability, or some combination of the two. Regardless, studies have shown that people with high EQ experience less stress, have greater mental health, perform better at work, and are more successful as leaders. Goleman indicated that EQ was the single most important skill possessed by successful leaders, and that it was twice as important as their intelligence quotient (IQ) or technical expertise.

In practical terms, this means having an awareness of our emotions and the emotions of others influences our behavior and impacts people in both positive and negative ways. Learning how to manage those emotions may be one of our greatest assets in personal and professional life. When considering self-presentation, or encoding the image we wish to project to others, the importance of EQ becomes apparent.

When viewing the behavior of others, the socially astute or high EQ observer may notice inconsistencies in others' communications. In their message-decoding they may look beyond the explicit intent of the performance (how another wants to be perceived) and examine the implicit intent of the performance (why they want to be perceived that way). The critical audience member may even decode that the performer is communicating something else, something that is equally observable to the explicit performance, yet more difficult to manipulate than words from the "script." These more visceral and less controllable forms of the performance are the non-verbal signals the actors call upon to enhance the performance.

When the "script" and the non-verbal signals are consistent, the performance is more convincing. To the extent there is a disagreement between the "script" and the non-verbal signals, we may detect an asymmetry in the performance, and do not find the actor convincing. Seeking authenticity, the great performers ensure that a performance has *symmetry* and that they can perform with that symmetry across a wide range of different performances. This is EQ in action.

Scientists have long been interested in studying emotions, and defining them based on core dimensions has been the most enduring approach. Most dimensional models incorporate some measure of valence (pleasantness) and arousal (intensity of feeling). Perhaps the most common of these dimensional models is the *circumplex model of emotion* developed by James Russell.[3] This model arranges emotions in a two-dimensional circular space, utilizing *valence* (pleasant – unpleasant) and *arousal* (degree of intensity) as the core dimensions of all emotions. In this model, emotional states can be represented or plotted at varying levels of valence and arousal depending on the degree of pleasantness and intensity of the emotion.

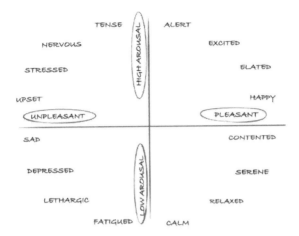

Figure 11: Russell's Circumplex Model of Emotion

Named as one of *Time Magazine's* 2009 "100 Most Influential People in the World," Psychologist Paul Ekman pioneered the study of emotions and how they are expressed. He and his colleagues created a taxonomy of over 10,000 facial expressions and conducted seminal research on the universality of physical expression of specific emotions. The result was the Facial Action Coding System (FACS) which associates and catalogues observable facial movements for every emotion.[4]

Ekman identified the bases of all emotions as anger, fear, disgust, sadness, and happiness. He suggested that these five basic emotions are connected viscerally to specific facial expressions and that they provide clear signals to those who recognize them. Similar to the point on authenticity and symmetry, Ekman, argued that "micro-expressions" could be used to effectively detect deceptions. A micro-expression occurs when both an intentional and an involuntary emotional response occur at the same time and in contradiction. Occurring in a fraction of a second when the brain generates an emotional response that the individual wishes to conceal. The result is a very brief display of the true emotion followed by the performed or desired emotional reaction. Timothy Levine, a Professor in Communication, and his colleagues have conducted groundbreaking research on deception and our ability to detect it.[5] They argued that when there is mismatch (asymmetry) between verbal message and non-verbal signals, an attribution of dishonesty is made. The problem with this, as he has discovered, is that the attribution is made even if deception is not present. In other words, when we encode our emotions for others, we do so with the understanding that there are norms and expectations for which displayed emotions are appropriate.

So, if we are encoding emotions for others' consumption, it begs the question, what is the self we are trying to present? Aristotle once said "Anybody can become angry – that is easy, but to be angry with the right person and to the right degree and at the right time and for the right purpose, and in the right way – that is not within everybody's power and is not easy." Aristotle was referring to the presentation of anger.

Irving Goffman first introduced the notion of *dramaturgy*.[6] He argued that the self is not some pure entity cloaked in our performance, or even the cause of the scene; rather, he suggested that the self is the product of the scene that is acted out. This includes the perception that other individuals have of the role we have played, the perception that we ourselves have of the role we played, and the collective perception that multiple others have of the role played. Therefore, we are at once many things to many people including ourselves.

This multitude of selves suggests that the presented self defies a singular distinction. A socially designed entity means that it is as much a product of our social surroundings as it is a product of our own design. As we adjust our behavior to be "appropriate" for a certain situation, we are presenting a different version of ourselves, which may or may not be authentic, and at least some of that presentation is defined by the social situation itself. The problem with having presented selves that are significantly different from our other presented selves is that we run that risk of diluting any sense of real self and thereby can become "socially diluted" or at least be perceived by others as being inconsistent in our performances and therefore insincere.

This "social dilution" was called *multiphrenia* by Kenneth Gergen. Gergen in his 1991 book, *The Saturated Self,* argued that we experience multiphrenia when we split the individual (or self) into a multiplicity of selves.[7] The condition, even more relevant today due to technologies that increase social contact, is the result of being simultaneously pulled in multiple and conflicting directions. His point was that each of these "pulls" represent a self-investment, and that each of these self-investments then compete for our time and attention, thereby causing a dilution, if not the dissolution, of the self. He also suggested that there were three "symptoms" that may indicate when an individual was experiencing this multiphrenia. He listed an increasing appetite of wants; increasing feelings of inadequacy; and increasing inner-conflict as indicators that a person was experiencing multiphrenia.

An increasing appetite of wants is the result of the multiple selves all needing symmetric performances and these symmetric performances need cognitive attention. This demand on our cognitive attention serves to reduce our ability to "not want" (because every want represents one less not want). The result is in an expansion of goals – of musts, wants, and needs. All of these goals demand some attention and personal energy as we pursue them or even merely desire them. Some of these wants demand more of our cognitive resources than others as we exert effort and encounter frustrations. Each subsequent new want then further reduces our liberties by increasing the demand placed upon our already limited cognitive resources.

This can lead to the second symptom of multiphrenia: an increased sense of inadequacy and seepage of self-doubt into our cognitive self. Essentially this is the result of bounded rationality and reflects the limitation that we do not have the ability to play every role to perfection, so with each performance there is compromise, which can result in asymmetry. As one performance impedes upon the authenticity of another performance, we have to make compromises between them. As we give attention to the needs and wants of one self, we must deprive another. This results in feelings of inadequacy in the neglected self. This sense of inadequacy is the result of populating ourselves with multiple selves that have competing demands and maybe even opposing ideals.

Lastly, increasing inner-conflict is the result of our conflicting selves. How we understand who we are is a vital product of social participation. To be perceived as socially desirable by others, our behavior must conform to certain socially constructed prescriptions and proscriptions. Yet, as with the range of our multiple selves, the validity of each socially defined self is threatened. In other words, what may be a socially appropriate self in one relationship may be completely inappropriate in another. The result is inner-conflict as we try to sort through competing expectations, values, and beliefs.

As previously discussed, we learned how to present ourselves when we were young. We quickly learned that inconsistencies in our performance made others think we were insincere. We learned that we acted differently around our friends than we did at home, and different yet again to how we acted in the classroom. We learned that all of these "selves" were, in fact, sincere, yet they were different. We "acted" differently in different situations. We sometimes presented variations of our different selves.

So, what are the implications of the contemporary presentation of self, where the self is an amalgam of selected photos, quotes, profiles, and 280-character dialogues? What are the social and – perhaps more importantly – psychological implications for the self in the often-superficial realm of social networking and insulated communication? Has the standard for a symmetric performance changed? How are stages, scripts, and props different in the digital domain? How is audience reaction and interaction different? Where is the line between presentation and deception? Finally, how is all of this changing the nature of social learning and knowledge?

A bona fide leader is a sophisticated interpreter of others' emotions and their presentations. Displayed emotions are a form of communication and the decoding of the emotion's meaning results in empathy. Similar to the discussion on empathy, the ability to accurately read others and respond with situationally appropriate behaviors establishes credibility and enhances trust. The result is a perceived sense of sincerity that enhances followers' confidence in leader motives and intentions.

The Meeting

The director was always nervous before this type of meeting. She knew she had to be convincing and could not make any mistakes. She had in the past and the result had not been pretty. A poor performance today would undermine her credibility and effectiveness. The future of her division was at stake. The quarterly sales were significantly lower than expected and she knew that if significant improvements were not made soon, major personnel changes would certainly occur.

She dressed conservatively yet stylish in a black business suit with a white blouse. Her hair was pulled back in a "let's get to work" no-nonsense style. Carrying her black leather portfolio and precisely on time at 9:00am, she briskly walked into the meeting room which was already filled with the sales managers. Showing no emotion, she took her seat at the head of the long conference table; all eyes were on her in anticipation of what was to come.

As she began to speak, she projected the most subtle of expressions; the look of anger and disappointment was not lost on the managers. She began with what had been the sales projections. She discussed the metrics behind those projections and defended the calculus. She then transitioned into the actual performance measurements and projected even greater angst. Inside she was still a bit squeamish – she knew this had to be a "spot-on" performance, or she and many of the managers would be history.

When she transitioned to what steps were needed to remedy the disappointing sales, she felt her performance was working. In fact, she was actually becoming angry. She was professional enough to be restrained, but her anger was actually palpable. She knew she had their attention; they were taking notes and offering suggestions for improvement. She was in control.

As the meeting came to a close, she was exhausted. Now she thought about it, she was always tired. The performance had sapped her. Yet she couldn't help but wish her friends could've seen it. They would not recognize the steely executive persona, all they knew was the happy, go-lucky friend. Her husband would be particularly surprised because he knew she almost always projected a somewhat diminutive or shy persona in social settings. Of course, all of these were a performance to some degree and all equally exhausting. Life would be so much simpler if they were just all the same.

Reflections

What was the presented self that the director displayed?

What were the props, costumes, and scripts?

What was the stage?

Was this a deception?

What are your performances?

What are your perceptions of who you are?

Do you experience symptoms of multiphrenia?

References

1. Barker, J.N. and W. Scott, *Marmion, or, The battle of Flodden Field a drama in five acts*. Lopez & Wemyss' ed. The acting American theatre. 1826, Philadelphia: A.R. Poole and Ash & Mason. 62 p.

2. Goleman, D., *Emotional intelligence*. 2005, Bantam Books: New York.

3. Russell, J.A., *A circumplex model of affect*. Journal of Personality and Social Psychology, 1980. **39**(6): p. 1161-1178.

4. Ekman, P., W.V. Friesen, and J.C. Hager, *Facial action coding system*. 2002, Salt Lake City, Utah: Research Nexus.

5. Levine, T.R., et al., *Sender Demeanor: Individual Differences in Sender Believability Have a Powerful Impact on Deception Detection Judgments*. Human Communication Research, 2011. **37**(3): p. 377-403.

6. Goffman, E., *Theœ presentation of self in everyday life*. Doubleday anchor book. Vol. 174. 1959, New York [u.a.]: Doubleday.

7. Gergen, K.J., *Theœ saturated self*. 2000, New York, NY: Basic Books.

PART TWO

INTERSPECTIONS

Part Two explores the space of social interaction. Armed with our introspections, we move into the dyadic space and beyond; in other words, the collisions that occur when our unique selves interact with others. We examine the power that social roles and role-sets have in influencing our behavior and how our personal reputations are formed and leveraged. We look at the critical nature of trust, the types of trust and the importance of social exchange. We consider what it means to be in a relationship and the necessary conditions of relations. We look at the collection of relationships and consider social capital as a tangible asset. Persuasion is presented as a very sophisticated form of communication. Finally, power is discussed from the perspective that it is fundamentally a dependency and ultimately we are in control of those dependencies.

Being bona fide means we must understand how our behavior influences others and how their behavior influences us. Having an accurate assessment of what others think of us is central to regulating our own behavior. To understand the nuances of social life (i.e., how to read social cues and how to emote in situationally appropriate ways) it is critical that we appreciate the notion of reciprocity and trust.

CHAPTER 7

Managing Impressions

"The self, then, as a performed character, is not an organic thing that has a specific location, whose fundamental fate is to be born, to mature, and to die; it is a dramatic effect arising diffusely from a scene that is presented, and the characteristic issue, the crucial concern, is whether it will be credited or discredited."

—Erving Goffman[1]

"Impression management," a concept originally introduced by Erving Goffman, refers to the deliberate process by which people attempt to influence how others perceive them.[1] This differs from self-presentation which takes the position that we are all actors emoting and projecting personas in near real-time, responding to cues from others, and responding in turn, with situationally appropriate behaviors. Most of the social behavior in the presentation of self is not even obvious to the actor. This is the primary difference between *self-presentation* and *impression management,* unlike self-presentation, which we could characterize as social desirability behavior, impression management is a deliberate and ongoing "bending" of the truth in order to make a specific impression. Indeed, self-presentation can be viewed as a tool or skill to be leveraged in impression management. As such, impression management can be placed on a continuum between self-presentation and deception, but its exact placement may not be possible because only the "actor" knows for certain the degree to which the performance is bending the truth.

In social settings such as our role-sets, we are often judged on our appearances. Successful players quickly learn to cultivate ongoing images of themselves for others' consumption. Whether the image is that of "team player" or threatening antagonist, managed impressions create a real social effect. An avid impressionist takes stock of their image and displayed behaviors, viewing themselves almost as an object. Then they consciously select from their repertoire of behaviors those that will best deliver the performance they desire.

The idea is that we all have a repertoire of behaviors, learned through our life experiences, and that we *manage* them deliberately. We consciously choose from a range of behavioral options that we think will best accomplish what we are trying to achieve. What is the motivational force behind this choice? What are we hoping to achieve with this behavior? What makes us believe our behavior will be received by others as we intend it to be? Will our behavior be the right behavior for the situation? To answer these questions, we'll revisit a theory that is useful in understanding human choice: expectancy theory.

Victor Vroom argued that *expectancy* is the belief that some degree of effort (behavior) will result in some degree of effect, and that this effect positively enhances the chance of attaining some desired outcome. Remember this is predicated by the value or *valence* the individual has placed on attaining the desired outcome. This self-assessment is based on past experiences, self-confidence and self-efficacy, and an assessment of the level of difficulty associated with attaining the goal. Vroom called this *instrumentality,* or the probability that the chosen behavior will be instrumental in attaining the goal.[2]

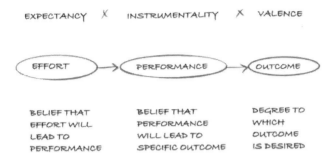

Figure 12: Vroom's Expectancy Theory

To better understand *impression management* we must begin with the understanding that it is a chosen, scripted behavior with a specific desired effect in mind. Using expectancy theory, we can ask: "What outcome am I trying to achieve? How much do I value that outcome? Will my behavior result in that outcome? Can I perform the chosen behavior?" Obviously a successful impressionist must know well how they present themselves, but they must also know something about their audiences. They must know how others perceive their behavior. Is their behavior appropriate for the context? Is it viewed in the manner the impressionist intended? Consider that the impressionist has free choice to display a range of behaviors for audience effect. What then are the categories of impression behaviors to choose from, and who are they directed at?

Also consider the levels of sensemaking (intra-subjective, inter-subjective, generic-subjective, and extra-subjective) and how our sense impacts what we value, how we assess our instrumentality, and our expectations. Revisiting Bandura's reciprocal determinism (self, action, and others), consider how surprises or miscalculations in what we value, how we assess our instrumentality, and what we expect, can result in new sense that in turn influences future behavior.[3] It has long been asserted that impression management behaviors are ubiquitous in organizational life.[4] These tactics are used to control the information presented to others in a manner that will result in the desired impression of the actor or impressionist.

Emotional intelligence informs us how best to control and express our emotions when managing our impressions, and how to interpret the impression management efforts of others. Impressionists use tactics to influence their bosses, subordinates, and their peers. Managers can use different impression management tactics for different effect. They may wish to be viewed as loyal by their superiors, strong by their subordinates, and competent to their peers. This can be accomplished by displaying desired organizational behaviors to superiors, stern or intimidating behaviors to subordinates, and emphasizing professional attributes and competencies to peers.

Impression management is a subtle manipulation of the information presented to others for a calculated effect. It is a performance specifically chosen to affect some outcome or behavior from an audience. Researchers have shown that certain tactics are better than others, depending on context and desired impression, and that some tactics can be blended for greater effect. But in general they agree that the numerous and specific behaviors and tactics that impressionists utilize can be grouped into five broad categories, as first suggested by Edward Jones and Thane Pittman. Jones and Pittman identified the five broad groupings of impression management behaviors as: *ingratiation, exemplification, intimidation, self-promotion,* and *supplication.* [5]

The *ingratiation* tactic is used when individuals wish to be viewed as likable. The behaviors range from self-deprecation to ego inflation of target others. This tends to place the actor in a one-down position relative to the target.

Exemplification is chosen when an individual wishes to be viewed as the dedicated employee or a model organizational citizen. This managed image plays the part of staying late, helping others with their work, taking work home, etc. From a power perspective, this tends to place the actor in a subtle one-up position relative to peers, but may reinforce a one-down position with superiors.

Intimidation is for when individuals wish to appear dangerous or threatening. Behaviors can range from verbal confrontation, body language, or even reputation management. Obviously this tactic overtly seeks to establish a one-up position.

The *self-promotion* tactic is used when an individual seeks to showcase their competence, or influence others' positive perception of their competence. Behaviors range from boasting to or more subtle approaches such as proximity or reference. This tactic is clearly used to establish a one-up position.

Finally, *supplication,* which is essentially the opposite of exemplification, is used when individuals wish to be viewed as in need of assistance or somewhat less capable than they actually are. The behaviors range from self-deprecation to feigned incompetence. Similar to ingratiation, this tactic will typically place the actor in a one-down position relative to the target.

ONE UP / ONE DOWN	IMPRESSION MANAGEMENT TACTICS	SEEN AS
−	INGRATIATION	LIKABLE
+ −	EXEMPLIFICATION	DEDICATED
+	INTIMIDATION	THREATENING
+	SELF-PROMOTION	COMPETENT
−	SUPPLICATION	WEAK

Figure 13: Jones and Pittman's Impression Management Tactics

In addition to specific behaviors, impressionists make use of the full range of tools at their disposal. They use tools such as clothing, hairstyles, body language, general behavior, and verbal or written communication, etc. They are sophisticated encoders that manage body language to project confidence or conceal anxieties. They choose words to manage truths or untruths. They choose to share or not share information. They exaggerate desired perceptions and downplay undesired perceptions.

We can view impressionists as "the other person," not ourselves. However, we all manage our behavior and leverage our EQ for the purpose of manipulating the impressions others have of us. Perhaps more interesting is that we expect others to do the same. In fact, we may actually think less of an individual if we suspect they are not actively managing their own impression. What would that tell us about what they think of us? That they think so little of us that they do not care what we think?

Industrial organizational psychologists (such as Dennis Organ) interested in understanding why some people at work consistently behave in a positive manner have identified a range of behaviors collectively called Organizational Citizenship Behaviors (also known as OCBs).[6] As proposed by Organ, OCBs are defined as those workplace behaviors that are not specifically rewarded, nor are there sanctions for not exhibiting them. OCBs are not part of an employee's job description, and are behaviors that employees do not receive training to perform. Organ suggested that there are five distinct OCB dimensions: *altruism, generalized compliance, sportsmanship, courtesy,* and *civic virtue.*

Organ argued that each dimension is a distinct set of behaviors that can be present in isolation or in concert with the others, but that in general and over time OCBs have a positive impact on others in the workplace and on organizational performance. He defined "altruism" as those behaviors that are directed at helping a co-worker. "Generalized compliance" refers to exceeding production, quality, or enforceable work standards. "Sportsmanship" is the general tolerance of job nuisances and having a good attitude in general. "Courtesy" is described as checking with others before doing something that would affect their work. Finally, Organ suggested that "civic virtue" was active involvement in company extramural affairs such as planning the holiday party.

So, how do we distinguish "authentic" OCB behaviors from impression management behaviors? Mark Bolino, a Professor of Management, suggested that the only way to determine that a behavior was chosen for effect, rather than being the authentic behavior of the performer, is to consider the behavior from the perspective of five different variables: *magnitude, audience, type, target,* and *timing.*[7] To begin with, "magnitude" refers to the significance of the behavior, such as coming in on a Saturday afternoon during a beautiful spring day to help a supervisor finish an important report. Compare that behavior with staying a little late on a rainy Thursday afternoon. "Audience" refers to who is witness to the behavior. While the supervisor may be the "target," co-workers may observe the behavior and make their own attributions. "Timing" refers to the impact of the behavior relative to impact at a different time. For instance, helping the boss with the report the weekend before a visit from the company president would likely be a better received behavior than helping during a routine period. Finally, the "type" of behavior demonstrated will have different effects. Bringing in coffee and doughnuts for a meeting will have a different effect on certain co-workers than coming in on that beautiful Saturday afternoon.

The point that Bolino makes here is that if in our consideration of behavioral choices, we make our decision based to some degree on how big the behavior is (magnitude), who is watching (audience), what the behavior is (type), who it is specifically directed at (target), when it is to occur (timing), or any combination of those variables, then we are involved in impression management.

Finally, and similar to the discussion on self-presentation, impression management benefits the impressionist (or us) in two basic ways. First, we benefit from the tangible results of our behavior – that is, how others perceive us. This can lead to positive outcomes such as success at work and placing us in a position to influence others. It plays into all of our sensemaking and ways of knowing. It can deliver us from the pain of embarrassment and put us in a place of security and influence. Second, how we present ourselves to others can impact how we perceive ourselves. The sum of our managed impressions can bring into focus how we view ourselves. As Goffman suggested, this dramaturgical perspective or "meta-identity" (what we think others think of us), becomes who we are to the world. He also suggested that over time we buy into our own performances and the *presented self* then influences the *cognitive self* and we become the sum of our performances. Perhaps OCBs cannot exist within the "selfless" definition provided by Organ and others, and are simply forms of the impression management tactic of exemplification.

Leaders are often, but not exclusively, the target audience of impression management efforts. It can take the form of "yes-people" (ingratiation) trying to win the favor of leadership by being very agreeable to an individual and highlighting their own accomplishments (self-promotion). Regardless of the tactic, a bona fide leader sees it for the performance that it is and does not easily yield to the manufactured impressions that have been presented. Similarly, authentic leaders are subtle and judicious in their use of impression management tactics because they are keenly focused on being viewed as authentic, and know that clumsy impression management attempts undermine this authenticity.

Hallway Trash

Jim was aware that his boss was in the hall behind him. He had heard him come out of his office as he had turned the corner. He always left for the weekly managers' meeting at precisely 5 minutes before 2:00pm. This was not lost on Jim. He was pretty sure the boss did not know that Jim was aware of his presence. As Jim spotted the candy wrapper on the floor ahead, he thought to himself that this was a great opportunity to show the boss what a great employee he was. He bent over to pick up the trash, never looking back, as if oblivious to his boss 20 feet behind. He smiled to himself. To look back would appear like he was only doing it because he knew the boss was there; his boss had to think Jim was authentic in his behavior.

Reflections

What do you think of Jim's behavior?

How do you feel about what Jim was thinking?

Do you think Jim intentionally placed himself in the hall at this time?

Do you think Jim placed the candy wrapper in the hall?

What type of impression management behavior was Jim engaged in?

How might this episode be viewed from Bolino's magnitude, audience, target, type, time perspective?

References

1.   Goffman, E., *Theæ presentation of self in everyday life.* Doubleday anchor book. Vol. 174. 1959, New York [u.a.]: Doubleday.

2.   Vroom, V.H., *Motivation in management.* 1965, American Foundation for Management Research: New York.

3.   Bandura, A., *Social learning theory.* 1977, Prentice Hall: Englewood Cliffs, N.J.

4.   Liden, R.C. and T.R. Mitchell, *Ingratiatory Behaviors in Organizational Settings.* Academy of Management Review, 1988. **13**(4): p. 572.

5.   Jones, E.E. and T.S. Pittman, *Toward a General Theory of Strategic Self-Presentation. .* 1982, Lawrence Erlbaum.: Hillsdale, NJ:. p. 231-261.

6.   Organ, D.W., *A Restatement of the Satisfaction-Performance Hypothesis.* Journal of Management, 1988. **14**(4): p. 547-557.

7.   Bolino, M.C. and W.H. Turnley, *Measuring Impression Management in Organizations: A Scale Development Based on the Jones and Pittman Taxonomy.* Organizational Research Methods, 1999. **2**(2): p. 187-206.

CHAPTER 8

Understanding Social Roles

"The notion of the role-set reminds us, in the unlikely event that we need to be reminded of this obstinate fact, that even the seemingly simple social structure is fairly complex."

—Robert Merton[1]

Social networking is often presented as a critical path to personal success, and while there is truth in that assertion, building and maintaining a network represents a significant investment in personal resources and sacrifices of individual freedom. We all have multiple networks that we belong to and maintain. And the line-up and composition of those networks is constantly changing and shifting. But when aggregated, they fuse to create a single map of all those people with which we are connected.

This aggregated result is called "social capital". Chapter 12 is devoted to this topic, but as a backdrop to the present discussion on social roles, we will say that social capital is a tangible influence asset that results from the connectivity or access an individual has with other individuals and groups. The result is a resource that individuals obtain through their relationships with others, and a social identity that comes with being in those relationships. Therefore, an individual's social capital can be defined as: *All those people and networks with which we interact – such as family, friends, neighbors, co-workers – that when taken all together, create an interconnected social system.* Within this overall system, are multiple sub-units known as "role-sets."

Role-sets (a term first coined by sociologist Robert Merton), are typically defined by the context that bring the members together, such as work (co-workers), geography (neighbors), family, friends, groups, and teams.[51] A role-set represents the set of individuals that are socially interconnected within a specific activity. It is typically a small social unit where members benefit from streamlined communication (encoding and decoding is easier), shared information, and a degree of trust above that of non-set members. We all have multiple role-sets to which we belong, as they consist of all of the people we work or interact with on a regular basis within the multiple contexts that define us. In other words, each of our role-sets includes all the people who value the benefits of belonging to that group.

To belong to a role-set and benefit from its membership, an individual must subscribe to certain behaviors that are widely accepted and expected by the members of that set. These expectations, or prescriptions and proscriptions for member behavior, serve to inform and constrain individual behavior within set boundaries, as defined by the set. To remain a member of the role-set, a member must behave according to these expectations and properly play to their role. Substantial or frequent deviation from those expectations can result in sanctions (i.e., diminished communication efficiency, trust, or access to information), the redefinition of those expectations, or even expulsion from the role-set.

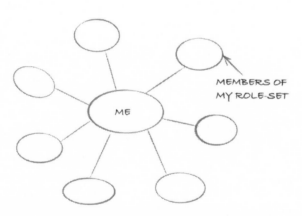

Figure 14: Role-set

Each of our unique role-sets has its own unwritten but well understood expectations governing the behavior of all of those in the network. These role expectations are sources of information regarding what behaviors, beliefs, and attitudes individuals within that specific network should do or have relative to his or her role within the network. These expectations can differ greatly from role-set to role-set. Consider the prescription and proscription differences between being a good neighbor and being a good co-worker. In the good neighbor role-set, sharing and borrowing of household items, social interaction, and mutual concern for property would be common expectations of that set. In contrast, good co-worker role-set expectations would likely be work-related and limited to those times and activities defined by the work context. If that means working a half-day on Saturdays is the norm, then it would be an expectation within that role-set that everyone shows up on Saturday mornings. Significant stress can occur when members of a role-set have different expectations, or when the expectations of one role-set interfere or are in direct conflict with the expectations of another role-set.

Daniel Katz and Robert Kahn, both noted sociologists, suggested that these role clashes occur when various members of a role-set impose different pressures on the individual.[2] When differences in these expectations are perceived, or even that those expectations differ from that of the perceiver, psychological conflict occurs. Katz and Kahn argued that we can experience several different types of role-set conflict. They suggested that role-set conflict falls into four basic categories: *intra-sender, inter-sender, inter-role, and person-role.*

"Intra-sender conflict" is described as conflict resulting from different and conflicting expectations from the same person within the role network. For instance, a supervisor at a supermarket demands that all customers be treated with the highest degree of respect. That means walking with customers to help them find a particular product, or taking the time to explain product differences to them. This same supervisor also expects a high degree of product placement and presentation of products on the shelves of the store. The store clerk now has conflicting expectations that must be resolved. To strive to fully achieve one expectation will undermine fully achieving the other. To remedy the distress, the worker must achieve equilibrium between the two expectations. Regardless, and similar to multiphrenia, a compromise of something less than full achievement of either expectation is the result.

"Inter-sender conflict" is when we perceive different expectations from different members in the role-set. To follow the retail store example, the clerk works primarily for two different shift managers. Most of the time the assistant managers work different shifts from one another, but on weekends and during busy holidays they are both on duty at the same time. The inter-sender conflict occurs when one manager emphasizes store cleanliness and customer relations while the other manager emphasizes maximum product placement on the shelves. When they are not present at the same time, the clerk can adjust her behavior to appease the manager on duty, but when the two managers are both present their differing expectations cause role-conflict.

"Inter-role conflict" occurs when we have different roles that partially overlap. Consider the clerk in our store. The clerk is promoted to shift manager. This position works directly under the assistant manager and is directly responsible for ensuring all of the other clerks do their jobs correctly. The new shift manager still considers herself one of the clerks but now has a new role, enforcing standards as one of the supervisors. Or consider the inter-role conflict that occurs when a non-work role and a work role collide, such as the working student under pressure to put in more hours at work, yet also striving to make good grades. In this example, each of the two roles are competing for dominance. In both of the previous examples, the competing roles are still active, yet both place differing expectations and prohibitions on behaviors.

Finally, with "person-role conflict," inner-conflict – or even cognitive dissonance – exists when the demands of the role contradict the values of the individual. For example, in our retail store, the new shift supervisor is under extreme pressure to not allow any employee to earn overtime. The assistant manager suggests having the employees clock-out at the end of their scheduled shift and then complete any unfinished work off the clock. The shift supervisor knows this is wrong and that it is even against the law, yet despite this and at her own discomfort she feels the pressure to meet the demand.

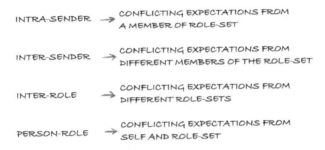

Figure 15: The Four Types of Role Conflict

All of these types of clashes are a source of role stress and they represent forces from the role-network exerting pressure on individual behavior. Katz and Kahn also suggested that every time we perceive differing expectations within our role-sets, we enter into a "role episode". A role episode is a sensemaking event. It begins with the set of prescriptions and proscriptions that are perceived in a given role-set. Awareness of these expectations can result in internal conflict, particularly when they are in conflict with other expectations.

Similar to cognitive dissonance, this internal conflict and must be resolved. Also, similarly to cognitive dissonance, there are essentially two choices: conform to the situation by redefining the "sense" and rationalizing the conflicting expectations, or maintain the current status quo which will invoke defensive behaviors to resist the change or conflict. Regardless, all levels of sensemaking are invoked as the network member continuously negotiates new expectations and prohibitions for themselves and others in the network.

Katz and Kahn also noted that "role uncertainty" exists when the expectations of a given role are not clear to the individual or they are unsure as to what it takes to be successful within that role. They suggested that there were two primary categories of role uncertainty, *expectation uncertainty* and *performance uncertainty*. Expectation uncertainty exists when an individual is not clear on what behaviors are valued within the role-set. Performance uncertainty refers to a lack of clarity on how others within a role-set perceive an individual's behavior relative to their expectations. The consequences of role uncertainty are similar to those of role clashes and include reduced performance, dissatisfaction, low self-confidence, sense of powerlessness, and increased stress.

A role-set that exists near or spans an external boundary with another distinct network, while of potential high value (as will be discussed later) is also associated with increased tension and perceived stress because the individual must deal with the resulting inter-role conflict. The role networks that are external to the first network often have demands and expectations contrary to those in the first, thus creating the inter-role conflict.

Attempts to exert power and influence over others may introduce role clashes and role uncertainty. A potential result is a negative change in attitudes and behaviors manifested in the form of conflict between network members. Ultimately this may lead to diminished trust, respect, and fondness within the role network. Interestingly, this decrease in network relations only serves to increase role uncertainty as the expectations within the network are embroiled in conflict. This conflict furthers blurs the clarity of the expectations within the network.

Within our various role-sets we often find ourselves in positions that exert power and influence over others, and in these situations we must be aware of the potential effects of the spill-over of our influence efforts. Every time we exercise power or exert influence, we are doing so either in contradiction to, or in affirmation of, existing role-sets. If we seek to introduce new expectations in a given role-set we must be aware of the potential negative impact on others' behavior and be on guard against making incorrect attributions regarding that behavior. If we are consistent with the expectations of the role-set, we must be aware of the impact that our expectations have within the network.

Additionally, our role-sets are continuously being redefined. This presents an opportunity for us to use sensemaking and influence to shape our role networks in the way that most benefits us. In other words, we can negotiate within our role-sets. As the role-set continuously morphs in response to changing organizational and environmental contexts, individuals are afforded opportunities to reshape expectations within their role-sets by resolving the clashes that will inevitably result. These "clash resolutions" then become the new expectations for behavior in the network. In other words, they become the new prescriptions and proscriptions for our behavior.

Finally, our role-sets represent the immediate "arenas" where social power dynamics are played out. This is where our reputations are formed. As individuals seek to renegotiate role expectations, interpersonal conflict may result. Even attempts to remedy the conflict may result in the perception of a power agenda by others. When conflict resolution is perceived as a power agenda, resistance to the resolution may follow. The result is a struggle between set members to establish new expectations for behavior within the network that most align with their interests.

In 1965, Bruce Tuckman suggested that as we adopt roles in small group or team settings, the team moves through specific stages of development.[3] He labeled these stages *forming, storming, norming, performing*, and later added *adjourning*. He proposed that transitioning through these stages is necessary and inevitable for teams to grow, meet challenges, solve problems, develop solutions, and ultimately be a successful results-oriented team.

In the first stage of team building, *forming*, individual roles form into a role-set. Individual behaviors and interests are supplanted by team behavior and interests. Individual behavior is largely focused on being accepted by the team and typically controversy and conflict are avoided. The focus of the various team members is on the dynamics of the team, its purpose for existence, goals and desired outcomes, what the various roles will be (both formally and informally), how things will get done and who will do them. This is the stage where members become acquainted, where roles are negotiated and where the role-set becomes explicit.

In the next stage, the *storming* stage, different ideas compete for consideration and inter-role conflict emerges. The members of the team begin to grapple with issues such as the common problems they are seeking to solve, how they will go about solving those problems, and who will lead them in solving those problems. At this stage, team members are becoming comfortable interacting and also more comfortable at voicing their opinions. As ideas and opinions are shared, inevitably the group members must navigate differences of opinion and competing attitudes. In some cases, this is short-lived and quickly resolved, yet in others it can become protracted and problematic. In fact, some teams never progress out of this stage. Yet the *storming* stage is necessary for the team to grow into a high-performing team.

As the team moves on from the storming stage and roles solidify, the team moves into the *norming* stage. In this stage, the team becomes focused on its purpose, the members settle into their individual roles, the prescriptions and proscription for member behaviors are accepted and adopted. In this stage, members establish norms for reciprocity, make decisions about when to assert themselves and when to compromise. In this stage, the sense of being a team, as well as individual role expectations within that team, are explicitly recognized. Also, in this stage, all team members feel a sense of responsibility and membership to the team and seek to work towards the achievement of the team's objectives.

While not all teams reach *performing* stage, it is the hallmark of high-performing teams. In high-performing teams, functionality is imbedded into the team's culture. Members coordinate and function in a cohesive manner and are able to achieve goals and objectives with little conflict or the need for outside supervision. In this stage, teams are characterized as being capable and motivated. The team members are now working together so well that they can make autonomous decisions, and while individual dissent is still to be expected, and in fact somewhat encouraged, it is managed as a functional aspect of the team's dynamics and channeled through means acceptable to the team.

Sustainment of a high-performing team is not a given – even high-performing teams occasionally revert to earlier stages when conditions change or team composition changes. In fact, many long-standing teams go through these stages in various degrees as their dynamics change. Additionally, roles change and are renegotiated, new prescriptions and proscriptions come and go, and the need for the team to remain intact may pass. In this latter scenario, Tuckman suggested that all teams eventually go through the *adjourning* stage, which essentially involves breaking up the team. This stage can be filled with mixed emotions, some happy, some sad, as the role-set dissolves.

A leader that cares about their followers understands that those followers are in multiple role-sets dealing with competing expectations. Leaders that understand small group dynamics are aware that their influence as a leader is unlikely to exceed the boundaries of the role-set. This is critical knowledge when managing change or implementing new ideas. The role-sets can dig in and be resistant to change or they can swing their weight behind the new. Bona fide leaders understand that the key to influencing the larger whole is in the trenches with the role-sets.

The Promotion

Rusty was tired all of the time these days. He longed for the way things used to be. Before he took the promotion his life was simple. He was simply the best programmer in the shop and everyone knew it. All he had to worry about each day was his own productivity. Since he had been promoted to the head of the programming department, all of that had changed. Firstly, his direct supervisor was constantly pressuring him to increase productivity, while at the same time expecting him to improve the morale of the department. Meanwhile, he was on a project team formed directly by the company's president. This team was charged with developing the future product line for the company. He wasn't sure why he was even on the team and for how long.

It had been an awkward adjustment to management for Rusty. As the team leader, he was now in charge of people he used to hang out and joke with. To joke around now would undermine his authority. He particularly dreaded going in today because he had to address a disciplinary issue within his own department. Two of the programmers that carpooled together were increasingly coming in late and leaving early. Additionally, they always seemed to be at odds with the other team members. Sometimes it seemed that they opposed others' ideas just to be difficult. Regardless, the other team members were looking to him to address their delinquency and negativity. He hated being in this role, but the others were expecting him to do something.

Reflections

What are some examples of role conflict from the story?

What are some examples of behavior prescriptions? Proscriptions?

What is likely the role episode that will follow?

How was role ambiguity presented?

What are the different roles in your life?

How are the expectations different between those roles?

What stage of team development was this team likely in?

What will be the impact on Rusty's social capital if he disciplines the bad actors?

What will be the impact if he does not?

References

1.   Merton, R.K., *The Role-Set: Problems in Sociological Theory.* The British journal of sociology, 1957. **8**(2): p. 106.

2.   Katz, D. and R.L. Kahn, *Theœ social psychology of organizations.* 2. print. ed. 1966, New York [u.a.]: Wiley.

3.   Tuckman, B.W., *Developmental Sequence in Small Groups.* Psychological Bulletin, 1965. **63**(6): p. 384.

CHAPTER 9

Personal Reputation

"So much depends on reputation – guard it with your life. Reputation is the cornerstone of power. Through reputation alone you can intimidate and win. Once it slips, however, you are vulnerable."

—Robert Greene[1]

Our social environments are filled with uncertainty. Every relationship, every role-set, every social interaction has some degree of attending uncertainty. We cannot be completely certain as to the future behaviors of others, and where there is uncertainty, there is some assessment of risk. This assessment of risk when considering the anticipated behavior of another person we can call "social interaction liability". When we perceive risk in a social interaction liability with another person, we look for ways to mitigate this risk by searching for more information to reduce our uncertainty. We do this by reflecting on our previous interactions, the opinions of others, and the image projected by the person within the social landscape.

As individuals, we ourselves wish to be afforded trust and status by others, so our goal is often to project an image of trustworthiness. In our professional lives, status is often signaled by proxy indicators such as pay, advancement, and professional position or title. As we strive for career success, we invariably interact with others in similar pursuits. This precarious social environment creates mutual dependencies among individuals as status is often determined through the perceptions of subordinates, peers, supervisors, customers, competitors, suppliers, etc.

As we leverage our EQ and interact within the context of our various role-sets, we are constantly crafting, maintaining, or defending our personal image. We can even suggest that all social influence behavior, or all self-presentations, are ultimately displayed for the purpose of maintaining this image. Every impression managed, every influence exerted, every political ploy undertaken, all seek the same end – to influence a desired effect or impression in the eyes of others. When these others then communicate their impression of our performances, they are like movie critics writing a review for a new release and being read by people that have not yet seen the movie. Their review and the sum total of all the other "critics" reviews then becomes our personal reputation.

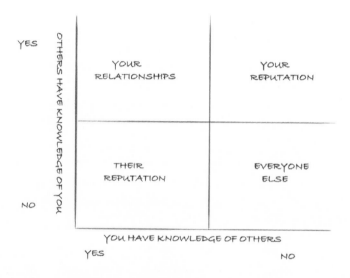

Figure 16: Personal Reputation

Personal reputation is the collective opinion of others. These collective opinions are communicated, shared, and distributed within and across members of those groups.[2] This reputation has real value to us in that others use it to form opinions of us before ever meeting us in person. They are essentially just trying to reduce their social interaction liability. The source of our reputation is the observed behavior by others of us within our various role-sets and, in turn, how that observed behavior is then interpreted by the members of that role-set. Paradoxically, while our reputation is formed within the role-set, the marketplace for the reputation is external to the role-set. This marketplace consists of other role-sets to which other members in our role-sets belong, but we do not. In this sense, reputation is an *informational commodity* and has its greatest value in places we may or may not even be aware.

When considering reputations from this informational commodity perspective, several points become clear. Firstly, reputations are a substitute for first-hand knowledge or experience with another individual. Secondly, when we enter into social arrangements with others, we take cognitive steps to protect ourselves emotionally. These steps include proceeding with caution, not revealing too much emotion, reserving affection, presenting a formidable image, etc. All of these presentations are our insurance against the uncertainty in new social encounters. The third point is that all of these presentations come at a cognitive cost. These costs, referred to as "agency costs," are related to protecting one's interests when entering into some arrangement with another.[3] The less we know about the other person, the greater the likelihood of increased agency costs. Finally, due to our bounded rationality, we are motivated to reduce those agency costs, and therefore naturally seek and accept information under conditions of uncertainty.

From this perspective, reputations represent a significant type of information. Although it is always and necessarily second-hand information, a reputation is an amalgam of opinions and observations of another regarding the sum of the performances of that individual. While we can also assign reputations to groups, teams, and organizations, for our purposes we will focus on personal reputations.

Most of the research to date on personal reputations has been conducted by Gerald R. Ferris and his colleagues.[4-7] In 2003, Ferris defined personal reputation as:

> A perceptual identity reflective of the complex combination
> of salient personal characteristics and accomplishments,
> demonstrated behavior, and intended images presented over

some period of time as observed directly and/or reported from a secondary source.[5]

This "complex combination of characteristics" can be a powerful force for establishing the social landscape between individuals that have yet to interact.

The idea that reputations are an important aspect of others' perceptions is not a novel notion or recent revelation. In fact, over 500 years ago, Niccolo Machiavelli in *The Prince* proposed that the reputation of the Prince was more important than the actual behavior of the Prince.[8] Recall Goffman's ideas on projecting image and the perspective of a "theatrical performance" where he suggested that the performance itself is what defines us. Implicit in this perspective is that an individual's reputation has value, can be crafted and, if threatened, vigorously defended through the management of our social performances.

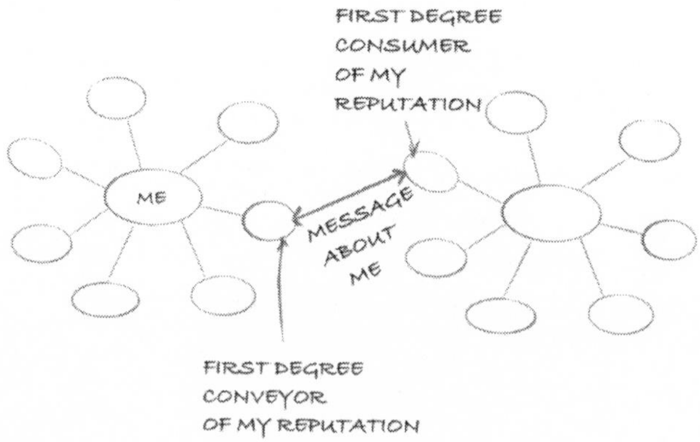

Figure 17: First-degree Reputation

An important distinction here is that reputation is formed by opinions at the first-degree of separation level. In other words, reputations are formed within role-sets or personal networks. Reputations are then communicated by the first-degrees to second-degrees, then second-degrees communicate the reputation to third-degrees, with degradation occurring at each successive degree. It is important to note that celebrity, fame, and infamy are different but related phenomena. The distinction can be made at the level of separation of the information conveyed – once the information conveyed is past three degrees of separation, we are likely approaching the threshold of celebrity, fame, infamy, and maybe even folklore. It's the realm of "a friend of a friend of a friend of a friend said…"

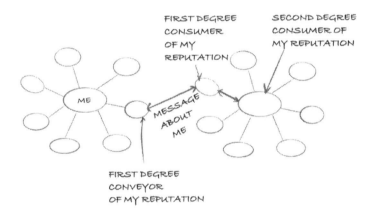

Figure 18: Second-degree Reputation

At a first-degree level, we will filter the information based on the source. If we are hearing it from a person we know to be generally pessimistic, we may discount their negative perspective accordingly. Similarly, if we know the source is biased in a particular manner, we may adjust their message to account for that bias. Also, veracity of the message will depend on the level of trust, credibility, and familiarity we have with the source.

Knowing how much fidelity is lost in message encoding and decoding, consider how much is lost at just the second-degree level. That's the "my friend said…" level. By the time I have the "message" it has been through two complete iterations of the communication model. Two encodes, two decodes, two instances of sensemaking and satisficing. Now think about a third-degree, the "I have a friend who has a friend that said…" We're not going to put as much merit in it, but it is information nonetheless, and if no other information is available then we may still consider it. It is likely that we will solicit more information from other sources and, depending on the extent to which all of the messages corroborate, we gain confidence in the information – in this case the reputation.

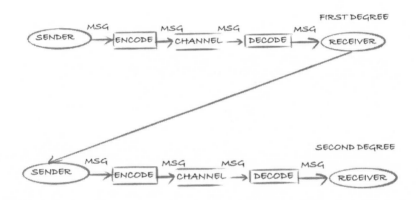

Figure 19: Reputation and Communication Model

Personal reputations need only be classified as positive or negative based on the perceived utility of the reputation to the decision-maker using it. Beyond that distinction, different types of reputation may very well be too numerous to label since reputation is defined by its context. Since a reputation is defined within a given context, assertive maintenance behavior is needed to firmly establish reputations in new contexts. Consider a situation where an individual is promoted from a lower level in the organization based on their reputation within that level. Failure to establish a new positive reputation at the higher level may result in an erosion of the original reputation at the lower level.

We can classify individual behaviors related to reputation maintenance as either assertive or defensive in nature. Our personal reputations are the perceived sum of all our actions and have taken a long time to construct and maintain, yet they are a fragile commodity. They can be rewritten in a moment. As previously mentioned, third parties and indirect ties are the corroborating forces behind reputations. Think of a reputation as a node in a network diagram in which the node representing the reputation has no direct connections. Rather the realm in which the reputation exists is only through indirect connections. These "reputational circuits" serve as enforcers, since bad behavior with any one member of the network will be reported to the other members, thus creating a deterrent against behavior inconsistent with expectations. Once a direct interaction occurs, first-hand knowledge supplants the second-hand reputational heuristic. Personal experience negates the need for the collective opinion of others.

When considering others' reputations during the process of making decisions, we are using the reputation as a "heuristic" approximation of trust. The use of heuristics is a cognitive strategy used to cope with complex information loads. Heuristics reduce the complex to a simpler form allowing for quick judgments and decisions. In a world of imperfect information and social interaction liability, in which decision-makers rely on heuristics to make rational assumptions regarding the intentions and predicted behaviors of others, the use of reputations in making judgments is commonplace. This serves to reduce the agency costs that come with uncertainty. From this perspective, reputation can be viewed as an expectation on future behavior based on previous actions. The power of a reputation lies in the degree of trust it can elicit from others. Therefore, the need for trust is the basis for the value of a reputation. It represents a belief that an exchange partner will not act in a self-interested manner at another's expense. The inherent value of this is in its ability to speed up decision-making and conserve cognitive resources.

If need for trust is the basis of the value of a reputation, then second-party conveyance (authority way of knowing) of the reputation is what legitimizes it. Indirect or second-party conveyances are a source of information which serves to enhance the trust one places in another. This triangulation effect on an individual's reputation increases the reputational costs of behaving in such a way that is inconsistent with the existing reputation. This serves as a kind of self-regulating mechanism. As we gain first-hand knowledge of another person, we contribute to (or detract from) their existing reputation when we speak of them to others. This triangulation effect on their reputation serves to increase or decrease the reputation's value among those others.

The greater the reputation's value, the greater the sanction is for violating the nature of that reputation. Similar to the forces in a role-set, this places certain prescriptions and proscriptions on behavior. The cost of violating the trust of a good reputation is a damaged reputation, which then results in less trust extended in future interactions. As previously mentioned, once we have established first-hand knowledge of a person, those experiences begin to supplant their reputation in our calculus. As we accumulate more interactions, the importance of the reputation fades further until we are left with actual trust or distrust based on that first-hand experience.

In a world where we are often defined – and even define ourselves – by the perceptions of others, our reputations represent real and powerful forces at play. The forces may be the symbolic meaning that is attached to reputation, or the sense that others make of us before they actually know us. We know that we can alter this sense through our collective presentations, but we can also alter this sense through the crafting and maintaining of our reputations.

While a reputation is the summation of a series of performances, the difference between reputation and self-presentation is that with self-presentation and impression management, the audience is known and the performance is directed at that audience. With reputation, the ultimate audience is unknown. Our reputations are "communicated" perceptions of our performances, not direct observations of the performances. The consumers of our reputation have not seen our performances, they have only heard of them. In this sense they are "secondary audiences" to our performances. If they do become a "primary audience" member at some point, our reputation may initially influence their own attribution processes as they seek to confirm the reputation that was communicated to them, essentially resulting in a *confirmation bias*.

A confirmation bias occurs when we look for behaviors that confirm the reputation that was communicated. We are primed to see them so they stand out to our observations. Consider when you get a new car, you suddenly see that make and model everywhere, whereas before you never really noticed. We also call this *priming*. Confirmation bias, also the result of bounded rationality, is the tendency to conserve resources by shortcutting the sensemaking process by seeking to confirm pre-existing beliefs or hypotheses, while largely disregarding alternative possibilities. Thus, actual perceptions of "primary audience" members are *primed* to either confirm or contradict the reputation that has been communicated to them. As they communicate their confirmation or contradiction to others still in the "secondary audience," they either reinforce or redefine our reputations and become an active agent in the reputation marketplace.

Conversely, when we ourselves are seeking to reduce agency costs in dealing with a new and uncertain social arrangement, we become the consumers of another's reputation. We assess their series of performances as relayed to us by others. We then assess who those others are and consider the merits of their assessments. In other words, the reputation of another results from a combination of the context of the situation, what we have heard from others, what we think of those others, and our own biases and experiences.

Finally, on the distinction between fame and reputation, fame represents a persona, whereas reputation represents interaction (behavior). Reputation and fame are distinctly different, as reputation represents second-hand perceptions of an individual's behavior as an informational commodity, whereas fame is a condition of being "known of" by many people. While famous people are often known of for their behavior, it is their persona that is famous.

A bona fide leader understands the value of their personal reputation. They understand that their reputation consists of a multiplicity of observed behaviors that have been reduced to a few salient characteristics. These prominent characteristics are then encoded, communicated and decoded all outside of the leader's ability to influence. Reputations have the potential to open doors that are not known, and throw up obstacles in paths not yet seen. Bona fide leaders understand that reputations are omni-directional which means everyone we interact with is a contributing author of our reputation. To a bona fide leader, everyone – regardless of position or status – is afforded the same degree of respect and dignity. Bona fide leaders also understand that the reputations of others are an imperfect composite of impressions. Bona fide leaders understand that they need to replace the *authority* way of knowing (established through the trust of others) with *reason* and *science,* and that is only accomplished by establishing trust.

The Negotiation

Marilyn could not fall asleep. Her mind was racing with indecision. First thing tomorrow morning she had to submit her request for the members of the negotiating team. She had one last position to fill and was undecided as to who she wanted. While she personally knew the other four members and was confident they would perform well and (perhaps more importantly) get along, the same was not true of the final position. She had never personally met the two people she was considering, but she knew of both of them.

Robert was known as a tough negotiator, one that you wanted on your side. Marilyn was aware of his successes in other negotiations and it was known that he did his homework and came well prepared. Marilyn also understood that Robert could be difficult to work with. Marilyn's good friend Wendy was Robert's boss and Wendy had shared with her the challenges of supervising Robert.

The other person she was considering was Kate. Kate was newer to the organization but was quite popular with her co-workers. Marilyn had heard that she was highly regarded by her peers and everyone seemed to like her. She was described as "very personable," as having "a great sense of humor," and as a "natural leader." The only concern that Marilyn had was her competence for this particular negotiation. She had heard from Jerry, a colleague of Kate's, that Kate had missed a few deadlines and had to correct several errors she had made in a report. Marilyn only knew Jerry as a fellow soccer parent on the weekends, but she did get the feeling that Jerry was in competition with Kate for promotion.

Marilyn felt that regardless of her decision, there would be challenges. Whether she would be spending time resolving conflict due to Robert's abrasiveness, or whether she would be spending time monitoring the timeliness and quality of Kate's work. She was just going to have to pick one and handle the consequences.

Reflections

What would you do if you were Marilyn?

What are her potential agency costs with Robert? Or Kate?

Which reputation do you feel is more accurate?

How might their reputations be reinforced?

How might their reputations be redefined?

What is your opinion of Marilyn?

What is your opinion of Jerry?

When will Marilyn no longer use their reputations in her decision-making?

References

1. Greene, R., *The 48 Laws Of Power*. The Robert Greene Collection. 2010, London: Profile Books.

2. Jazaieri, H., et al., *Content, structure, and dynamics of personal reputation: The role of trust and status potential within social networks*. Group Processes & Intergroup Relations, 2019. **22**(7): p. 964-983.

3. Jean, E., *Reputations, Trust, and the Principal Agent Problem*, in *Trust in Society*. 2001, Russell Sage Foundation. p. 185.

4. Blass, F.R. and G.R. Ferris, *Leader reputation: The role of mentoring, political skill, contextual learning, and adaptation*. Human Resource Management, 2007. **46**(1): p. 5-19.

5. Ferris, G.R., et al., *Personal reputation in organizations*. Organizational Behavior: A Management Challenge, 2003. **201**.

6. Hall, A.T., et al., *Leader reputation and accountability in organizations: Implications for dysfunctional leader behavior*. The Leadership Quarterly, 2004. **15**(4): p. 515-536.

7. Zinko, R., et al., *Toward a Theory of Reputation in Organizations*, in *Research in Personnel and Human Resources Management*. 2007, Emerald Group Publishing Limited. p. 163-204.

8. Machiavelli, N., *Theœ prince*. Theœ modern library of the world's best books. Vol. 49. 1940, New York: The moderne library.

CHAPTER 10

The Social Marketplace: Trust and Social Exchange

"Joy = Trust x Purpose."

—Paul Zak[1]

"If you don't trust those that work for you, they can't be trusted. If you do trust them, then they can."

—David Levy[2]

Trust is "assured reliance on the character, ability, strength, or truth of someone or something."[3] The single most important concept in organizations and in social existence is trust. Trust is a brokering mechanism we invoke when we interact with others. It turns solitude into social interaction. It allows us to engage with others in spite of our potential vulnerabilities. If our lives were completely devoid of trust, then we would never interact on any level with anyone else, our self-interest would dictate that we not expose our vulnerabilities and that we take advantage of others' vulnerabilities. We would be doomed to a life of complete and utter barbarism and solitude. Trust allows us to enter into social arrangements, friendships, relationships, business endeavors, and everything else in our life that involves other human beings. Of course, at its core, trust is also satisficing.

Trust has been studied extensively by social scientists seeking to better understand the construct. Typically, this research has been dominated by an assumed rationality of the decision-maker. Tom Tyler and Roderick Kramer, scientists interested in why and how we formulate trust, suggested that while this rational perspective has enhanced our understanding of trust, it has also restricted our understanding of how non-rational forces (such as social context) might impact trust.[4]

We all intuitively understand trust and how it works because we learned about it as children. For many of us, some of our most vivid childhood memories involved trust. Either earning someone's trust or someone earning ours, or breaking someone's trust or having someone violate ours. We can never have perfect information about another person, so at some point we get to a "good enough" place and allow for the interaction. We use a combination of logic or reasoning and social context to get to that "good enough" place. We satisfice.

From a logic perspective, trust is a calculus – a computation of a behavioral expectation of another person. This calculus-based trust is built on an assessment of what the other party stands to gain if they honor the trust, or lose if they break the trust. The assumption being that if the reward is great enough, or the deterrent is sufficiently painful, the behavior can be predicted. From a social perspective, our EQ becomes a very important capability as we operate on emotional faith that the other person will not take advantage of us. We call upon our life experiences, contextual factors, and emotions to help us "read" the other person in order to get to that "good enough" calculus.

But no calculus is a guarantee, since perfect information is not possible. We are always dealing with some degree of uncertainty because we are always satisficing. If we had perfect information, there would be no need for trust, there would just be certainty. In all things social, our information is imperfect, therefore requiring us to build a bridge of trust in interactions with others. These bridges, made of part logic and part emotion, take on different forms depending on the context of the interaction, the players involved, and the stakes of the interaction. To illustrate this, let's consider what trust looks like based on varying degrees of logic and social context. How does the nature of the trust change when we consider it from the most logical perspective compared to the most emotional? Using these two dimensions, at least five distinct forms of trust can be characterized: *transactional, interactional, relational, identificational* and *intuitional*. Each of these types of trust represents our sensemaking at work, and increasing degrees of satisficing occur as we move into more emotional calculus, as we seek to make assessments about the likelihood of another's behavior and conserve our cognitive resources.

Biases help us satisfice. They make short work of what is otherwise a labor-intensive endeavor. Biases arise when we use heuristics, or rules of thumb, as input into decision-making. However, heuristics can lead to biased decision-making as well. Conversely, we are cognitively limited (bounded rationality) as to how much logic we can apply in establishing trust, so we satisfice to varying degrees.

The first, and most rational form of trust, "transactional trust", sometimes referred to as deterrence-based trust, is mostly a logic-based trust that leverages some mechanism, such as a contract, to create a level of pain for one or the other in an agreement or relationship. This mechanism works to ensure that the pain is equal to or greater than the gain of violating the agreement or relationship. This type of trust is common in business arrangements where either party has little knowledge of the other and safeguards need to be put in place to ensure both parties are significantly committed to the agreement or arrangement. It is important to note, however, that these safeguards produce agency costs. In other words, it takes time and thought to craft and enforce the mechanisms that will ensure the transaction. Of particular note here is that it assumes rationality of all parties involved. That is why irrational thinking is so disturbing – we lose the ability to calculate transactional trust.

"Interactional trust," again mostly based on logic, is a type of knowledge-based trust that is built up over time. With interactional trust there is a history of interaction and more importantly, there is the promise of future interaction. This promise of future interaction serves as the primary governing mechanism in interactional trust. The potential punishment for violating trust at this level is the loss of future interaction. Assuming that both parties value that future interaction, they are discouraged from violating the trust because to do so would cost more than what would be gained in the violation. In other words, a small business owner could potentially pawn off a faulty product to an unsuspecting customer for a higher than normal profit, however, in doing so, the business owner has likely lost any future business with that customer.

"Relational trust," is also a knowledge-based trust, and is a result of significant interactional trust. Unlike interactional trust which places a greater emphasis on future interaction, relational trust is based more on emotional input and stems from a long history of past interaction. With relational trust, we have knowledge of and perhaps a personal relationship with the other party. This is social context. Through many previous interactions we have come to view the other party as predicable. This predictability serves as the trust mechanism in the exchange. As in all categories of trust, however, this trust can be damaged if violated and perhaps the emotional damage is greater here than with any other type of trust.

"Identificational trust," unlike the others, is mostly derived from social context and is based on personal biases. It does not necessarily rely on a guarantee, a promise of future interaction, or even a history of interaction. Unlike the other types of trust presented so far, identificational trust is based on a mutually recognized identity or role-set, not interaction. Heavily influenced by social context, this mutual identity makes us feel at one with the other party. This identity can come from similar experiences that are either shared or known, such as military boot camp, or from some recognized form of membership such as a school teacher. Whatever the identification, we see the other as similar to ourselves and afford them a certain level of trust purely based on that identification. This is known as the "similar-to-me bias" and can produce a high level of trust, yet be the least scrutinized. We simply trust others based almost exclusively on social context and without much logical consideration.

Finally, "intuitional trust" has very little logic calculus and is almost entirely based on emotions. This places an even higher premium on our EQ. The higher our EQ, the better we can read others and in turn make assessments of their trustworthiness with little more than a quick social interaction with them. It is not based on face-to-face interaction, rather it is based on something more visceral. It is that feeling we get, based on our entire life's experiences, that someone seems "OK." We can't put our finger on it, perhaps it's a certain ease of communication, or subtle nuances of communication style or self-presentation. Whatever it is, we find ourselves trusting someone relatively quickly with very little knowledge or previous interaction.

Obviously, our intuitional approach is not always right, and sometimes in retrospect we see the signals that we were blind to in the beginning. In fact, Timothy Levine, a Professor of Communication Studies, suggested that we may actually be more wrong than right due to "truth default theory" (TDT).[5] With TDT, Levine argued that most of the time we default to decoding communication (verbal and non-verbal) as being true – in essence, we have a bias towards communication being true. This becomes a problem when assessing trust largely from a social context because, as author Malcom Gladwell argued, science suggests that perfect matches between our expressions and our feelings are infrequent.[6]

But what if there is no first-hand knowledge or assessment and yet there looms the likelihood of a future interaction, such as the case of a new co-worker or incoming boss. As previously discussed, we then often turn to the individual's reputation. In this sense, we conjure up an informational trust. We afford trust based on the opinions of others or credentials or titles. Especially powerful are the opinions of those who we trust. In this sense, the individual's reputation becomes a surrogate for one of the types of trust previously discussed. This is the reason that reputations have value. Reputations can substitute, at least temporarily, for interactional, relational, and even identification-based trust. Similarly, a reputation can be measured by the degree of trust it elicits in others. From this perspective, indirect or third-party ties are a source of information which serves to enhance the trust one places in another in the absence of first-hand experience or information. This is why informational trust is difficult to place on the logic/emotion grid: because the sources of our information vary widely from highly trusted to highly suspect, thereby resulting in varying levels of logic and emotion.

So how do we get others to trust in us? Certainly we can see the value of our own reputations. It is like the bow wave in front of a boat – it precedes us and is caused by our actions. We can never quite touch it directly, yet our actions influence what it looks like and the general direction that it travels. We are not sure how far it will travel and who will feel its effects. So, our reputation is something that reflects how others see us, it precedes us, and we can influence it, yet not control it.

Setting reputation aside for a moment, how do we get others to trust us? It is through creating reciprocal exchange. In other words, establishing interactional trust allows for multiple interactions, which can then develop into to relational trust. This is actually the way influence is acquired in the absence of formal authority. Because people believe their actions will be paid back in some form or another, the basis for reciprocity is virtually always present.

Reciprocal exchanges can take on many forms. They can be tangible actions such as the sharing of resources or actual assistance with a project, or they can be less tangible things such as encouragement, admiration, or praise. Regardless of the form they take, exchanges are the basic principle behind all social transactions. It is based on the near-universal belief that people should be paid back for what they do. This belief has been held by primitive and sophisticated societies alike.

A challenge arises in the face of exchange relationships, however, for just as currencies are traded in the financial market, they are also traded in organizational life. There are so many types of currencies or payments that the range of what can be exchanged is infinite. These "currencies" are flexible because they provide multiple ways in which to express gratitude, give assistance, or reciprocate another's actions. However, the "rate of exchange" depends on how the receiver values the original act compared to the value of their reciprocal act. Those people that are good at this valuation, that is, they assess value in a way consistent with our own calculations, are those we find ourselves trusting more rapidly.

When considering relationships, we must consider the *norm of reciprocity*. This is a common social norm which says that if I give something to you or help you in any way, then you are obliged to return a similarly valued favor. Note that we do not necessarily expect the exact favor returned, just something that would approximate the value of the favor we extended. This norm is at the core of human existence. It is what allows us to live in proximity of one another and to develop civilized societies. It is universal across all societies and cultures and arguably is wired into our genetic code. It may, in fact, be akin to human instinct. That being said, how does that influence our behavior and the behavior of others?

Understanding the reciprocity norm helps us to know ourselves and know others better. Since I am not always able to reciprocate in kind, I therefore must find some way of reciprocating that approximates the value of the original good deed. This means I need to leverage empathy and EQ to come to a value assessment that is similar to the other person's assessment. Role-sets and their attendant norms play into this calculus, as do other contextual factors such as timing (i.e. staying late on a Friday night to assist a co-worker would likely be more valuable than staying late on a Monday night). To violate this accounting is to risk being ostracized for violating a social norm. Thus, at the heart of the reciprocity norm is social exchange.

All relationships are based on exchange. This give and take represents a constant "social bank account" that is either in surplus, deficit, or balance. *Social exchange theory* suggests that how we feel about a relationship with another person depends on our perceptions of our "social bank account" with them. This "bank account" exists based on trust and it contains a ledger in which the history of deposits and withdrawals has been recorded. In fact, one of the earliest contributors to social exchange theory, sociologist Peter M. Blau, suggested that social exchange and the principles of reciprocity were the bases of power relations in organizations.[7]

In valuating these deposits and withdrawals we use our sense, and the sense of others, to determine what is "fair." In deciding what is fair, we develop an "exchange rate" that we use to determine the value of a deposit or withdrawal, and these values differ based on the nature of the relationship within which we are doing the accounting. In this sense, the "exchange rate" is socially defined by those in the relationship or even within the role-set.

So how do we determine the exchange rates? What we exchange has a perceived value as determined by both the giver and the recipient. It can be emotional, such as a show of appreciation, or a more tangible tit-for-tat. The point is that we are tracking these exchanges and become aware of deficits or surpluses. In fact, we could say that trust is a delayed exchange, or the promise of reciprocation. A deposit made by one today with the expectation of a reasonable exchange rate calculation and a return deposit later. Without trust, social exchange is remanded to an immediate transaction and the exchange becomes one that is backed by formal guarantee.

Paul Zak, an economist who has also studied brain imaging and neurology, suggested that there are neurological mechanisms that enable cooperation, trust, and social exchange.[1] Specifically, he found that the more people perceived they were trusted by others, the more oxytocin their brains produced. As their oxytocin levels increased, the more likely they were to reciprocate by being more trustworthy. In other words, you have to trust to earn trust.

Trust is the primary enabler of a bona fide leader. Trust is the payoff for the authenticity. By being authentic, leaders remove all opportunities for asymmetry and invoke all of the types of trust. A bona fide leader is well aware of the different types of trust and is equally well-versed in leveraging all of them. From their reputations, to relationships, to first encounters, they are adroit at establishing trust swiftly and they honor that trust unwaveringly.

The Orma Tribe

In a study by Jean Ensminger, based on her anthropological fieldwork with the Orma tribe of Tana River District in Kenya, she illustrated that social governing mechanisms developed organically in relationships within the cattle business of Orma.[8] The cattle camps were often 100 miles away from the town in which the cattle owner lived. If no family members were available to assist managing the herd, the owners were faced with hiring other herders. Given the distance, a principal-agent dilemma arose between the owner and the hired herder.

Interestingly, trust relationships and social exchange have evolved as the most efficient means of reducing the associated agency costs between these two parties. To make the argument that trust reduces these costs, Ensminger illustrated that Orman cattle owners and herders often developed relationships of generalized reciprocity. She points to the paternal adoption of trustworthy herders by owners as evidence of this argument. This is the result of an iterative process that grew in opportunity costs for both the owner and the herder the longer the relationship exists. For the herder, the cost of shirking would result in losing the job and having to start over with a damaged reputation. For the owner, the cost of defaulting on payment would mean having to find a new herder while having the reputation of one who does not pay. Thus, both parties were incentivized to conduct themselves in accordance with the other.

Reflections

What type of trust was likely present at the beginning of the herder/owner relationship?

Did the type of trust likely change and to what?

How does the norm of reciprocity relate to trust?

How does reputation relate to trust?

What are the likely "currencies" of exchange in this situation?

What are likely the sanctions for not adequately assessing those currencies?

References

1. Zak, P.J., *Trust factor*. 2017, New York: AMACOM, American Management Association.

2. Levy, D., J. Parco, and F. Blass, *The 52nd Floor: Thinking Deeply About Leadership*. 2008.

3. *Merriam-Webster Dictionary*. [cited 2019 Web Page]; Available from: https://www.merriam-webster.com/.

4. Roderick, K. and T. Tom, *Whither Trust?*, in *Trust in Organizations: Frontiers of Theory and Research*. 1996, SAGE Publications, Inc: Thousand Oaks. p. 1.

5. Levine, T.R., *Duped: Truth-Default Theory and the Social Science of Lying and Deception*. 2020, Tuscaloosa, AL: University of Alabama Press. 1-277.

6. Gladwell, M., *Talking to strangers*. 2019, Place of publication not identified: Allen Lane.

7. Blau, P.M., *Exchange and power in social life*. 1964: J. Wiley.

8. Jean, E., *Reputations, Trust, and the Principal Agent Problem*, in *Trust in Society*. 2001, Russell Sage Foundation. p. 185.

CHAPTER 11

Interpersonal Relationships

"To understand relationships we must take into account the type of relationship, its diverse characteristics, the age and social class of the participants, their individual histories, the culture in which they live, and so on."

—Robert A. Hinde[1]

Interpersonal relationships, like people, defy simple distinctions. They are comprised of countless variables, including the individual characteristics of the people that comprise the relationship. Relationships are a dynamic social phenomenon, constantly changing and morphing continuously throughout their existence. But relationships, just like living organisms, have a punctuated existence. We can easily find their origin, we can easily describe their existence, and perhaps we can even acknowledge their termination.

Interpersonal relationships, which serve as the foundation for relational trust and are the source of our reputations, are host to the most pertinent aspects of social influence. Learned primarily through our life experiences, we seem to intuitively understand the relationships we are in because they are central to our daily lives and we have invested much emotion and energy into them. But if we stop to think about what a relationship actually is as a social construct, what do we know? We can quickly guess that interpersonal relationships have many degrees of complexity and involve characteristics that extend beyond the sum of the parts.

If we recall the notion of bounded rationality, we know that it would be impossible to examine every aspect of a relationship. Considering all the non-verbal communication, thoughts, intentions, emotions, feelings, history, etc., the variables are infinite and changing with every new interaction. So rather than try to examine relationships at the micro-detail level, perhaps it is useful to look at relationships from a broader perspective and identify characteristics common in all relationships.

Borrowing ideas from Robert A. Hinde, who researches interpersonal relationships, we can classify the primary dimensions of relationships, and show how they influence individual behavior and relate to the interpersonal dynamics.[1] Hinde suggested that there are five necessary conditions for a relationship to exist. First, it must be between two individuals, or at the *dyadic* level. Next, both members of the dyad must be aware of, and have perceptions of, the relationship dyad – one alone is not sufficient. Third, both members of the dyad must also have some expectation of the other and awareness that there is a reciprocal expectation of them. Next, both members of the dyad have an awareness of the relationship's existence over time. Finally, according to Hinde, the relationship is uniquely situated in a *context* or social setting.

Let's look at each of Hinde's dimensions in greater detail. First, an interpersonal relationship exists at the *dyadic level*. This is simply that an interpersonal relationship exists between two people. While there may be situations where a group of people come together socially, a unique interpersonal relationship exists *between* each dyadic pairing of the individuals in the group. A relationship does not reflect the characteristics of just one member, but rather it is a combination of the characteristics of both members. Consider how you would characterize the different relationships you are in. While you may describe two different people as being nearly identical in personality, you wouldn't necessarily characterize the two different relationships as nearly identical. Some people make us laugh, some make us angry, and some make us ambivalent or sad. This is due to the unique interactions we have had with that individual and in that relationship, and these feelings find their way into how we would characterize the relationship itself. Our assessment of one another within the relationship is complex and dynamic. Each member has a "sense" of the other, and this "sense" influences the attitudes, attributions, perceptions, and behaviors toward the other.

Second, for the relationship to exist at the dyadic level, both members of the dyad must be aware of the other and both have a "sense" of the other's "sense," which in turn influences how their own sense is made. In other words, an awareness of how the other makes sense of events becomes a part of the relationship itself. Consider a relationship where one individual always seems to take things the wrong way. No matter what is said, they seem to take it personally or in a manner that was not intended. How does that now affect the relationship in general? Now the other member of the relationship must either change their behavior to accommodate, or remain unchanged and risk conflict. Either way, just being aware of the other's sense impacts the relationship. Also, this mutual awareness characteristic means that if I have a strong admiration for another person and know a lot about them, but they have no awareness of me, then we do not have a relationship.

Third, both members of the relationship must have some expectation of social exchange. Both members have established an "account" with one another and have an expectation from the relationship. This social exchange or reciprocal expectation can range from friendship to task assistance to a mutually beneficial arrangement. Whether the relationship is based in attraction or financial gain, expectation of future interaction is critical. A relationship cannot exist without the promise of reciprocity, and both persons in the dyad must share this perspective. Interestingly, because relationships involve expectations of reciprocity, the magnitude and frequency of this reciprocity become a defining aspect of the relationship.

Fourth, both members are aware of the existence of the relationship over some continuum of time. A relationship has a history of interactions that over time come to affect expectations about future interactions. These expectations are based on the sense made by each party and they may be consistent or inconsistent with the perceptions and expectations of the other party in the relationship. These expectations are vulnerable to our attribution processes and our sense of understanding, and as a result they are loaded with all of the baggage we carry around. Our emotions, aspirations, sensitivities, hopes, fears, etc., are all imbedded in our unique expectations of future interactions within the relationship. That means that while each relationship is a fixed entity, in that it is unique to the dyad, it is also dynamic in that new history, and thereby new expectations are being written with every new interaction.

Finally, both members of the relationship are influenced, albeit differently, by the context within which the relationship exists. This context includes forces that come into play, such as past experiences in other relationships, perceptions of others, or even the very notion that the relationship exists among other relationships and role-sets, all come together to create a context from within which the relationship is nested. Consider how a relationship with one individual becomes a source of friction with another. The others in both of those independent relationships can be influenced even though they themselves are not in a relationship. For example, if we are in a relationship with someone who has a negative reputation, then others who we are in relationships with may perceive their relationship with us in a different manner.

So then how do relationships develop? One of the most influential models of relationship development was proposed by psychologist George Levinger. The model he developed suggests there are five stages to relationship development.[2] Each of these stages is distinct, and the transition from one to another it not necessarily gradual but can happen quite quickly. The five-stage model implies that interpersonal relationships are like living organisms and, as previously mentioned, quite complex and ever changing.

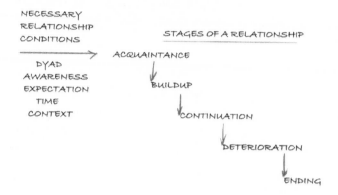

Figure 20: Conditions and Stages of a Relationship

Also, like all living organisms, Levinger suggested that relationships have a lifespan: a beginning, a maturation period, and an end. This is consistent with the idea that a fundamental characteristic of a relationship is that is exists on a time continuum. Relationships tend to grow and improve gradually, as the expectation of exchange with the other grows in frequency or significance.

The acquaintance stage – Becoming acquainted can occur many different ways. Two people can be introduced, can recognize each other through similar patterns of behavior, share certain experiences, or experience mutual attraction. Regardless, as they come together and recognize a mutual social exchange, they are entering into a relationship and the time continuum begins. At this point they simply share a *social object*. A social object is the reason that brings two people together in communication and will be discussed in next chapter in greater detail. At this stage it is not likely that much is known about the other, although others' opinions or even reputation may be present. If the relationship shows promise for future mutual social exchange and reciprocity, then continued interactions may lead to the next stage, but acquaintance can continue indefinitely and be the defining aspect of the relationship – one that has very little value or frequency associated with the exchange. Trust at this stage is likely to be identification-based, intuitive, or transactional.

The build-up stage – During this stage, interactional trust develops. As we extend greater trust based on a history of interactions, care and understanding develop as well. This is where we become more aware of the other's sense and that knowledge now becomes a part of the relationship itself. Strong feelings of liking and attraction may appear at this stage. Trust at this stage is largely interactional.

The continuation stage – At this stage both members of the relationship share an understanding that the relationship has a long future of interaction. Trust evolves from interactional trust into relational trust. We trust the other in the relationship because the promise and value of future exchange is much greater than anything gained through breaking the trust. That being said, violations of trust at any stage can lead to mistrust, but at this stage they are particularly devastating on the relationship and potentially lead to either of the following stages.

The deterioration stage – Not all relationships move to this stage. The relationships that do enter into this stage tend to be characterized as having decreasing trust or decreasing promise for future exchange. Trust may diminish or turn to distrust, conflict may increase, or ambivalence and disinterest may set in. Deterioration may happen suddenly, such as in a violation of trust, or gradually, such as when the promise of social exchange diminishes.

The ending stage – The final stage discussed by Levinger marks the end of the relationship, either by death in the case of a healthy relationship, or by separation. Arguably, however, the only time a relationship is truly terminated is when one or the other party no longer remembers the relationship. As mentioned at the beginning, what Levinger describes as the termination stage, may actually be nothing more than a good relationship that has deteriorated into a bad one. Consider that even a divorced couple that is incommunicado, and that mutually loathes one another, can still be characterized as being in a relationship – it is just not one characterized by positive reciprocity and trust.

Leader-Member-Exchange (LMX) theory is a relationship-based approach to leadership.[3] LMX focuses on the dyadic exchange relationship between leaders and followers. Foundational to this approach is that the relationships are based on mutual trust and have become relational trust. Bona fide leaders love their followers and develop real and lasting relationships with them. The resulting trust runs deep and is unifying. Authentic leaders understand the importance of building trust from the ground up, one relationship at a time, rather than top-down.

The Deli Guy

Jessica was a creature of habit. She followed her weekly routine without much deviation. Today was no different. She was on her way to the grocery store to stock up for the week. One of the things she always purchased was freshly sliced sandwich meats from the deli.

As with most routine activities, the people encountered in the routines become familiar faces. Sometimes so much so that it seems odd when you see them in a location other than the one in the routine. This was the case yesterday when she ran into the deli guy who was usually working on Sunday afternoons. She had always thought he was cute and of course he was always polite and courteous. But she suspected that perhaps he was a bit more courteous to her than the other customers. His eyes seemed to linger connected with hers for just a bit longer than was casual. Yet when she said hello to him the day before at the library, she couldn't be sure if he even recognized her.

The deli guy was on her mind as she made her way to the grocery store. This was not the first time either. In fact, it had been several months since she first noticed him. She would secretly hope that he would be working when she went to the store. She had even gone in the morning once only to learn he was not at work yet, so she made sure from that point onwards to go in the afternoons. She wondered if today he would say anything beyond the typical customer conversations. She sure hoped so.

Reflections

Using the necessary conditions for a relationship, explain why Jessica and the deli guy are or are not in a relationship?

How would we know if they were in the acquaintance stage?

How would we know if they were in the build-up stage?

How might we write the ending stage of this relationship?

References

1. Hinde, R.A., *A suggested structure for a science of relationships.* Personal Relationships, 1995. **2**(1): p. 1-15.
2. Levinger, G., *Toward the analysis of close relationships.* Journal of Experimental Social Psychology, 1980. **16**(6): p. 510-544.
3. Graen, G.B. and M. Uhl-Bien, *Relationship-based approach to leadership: Development of leader-member exchange (LMX) theory of leadership over 25 years: Applying a multi-level multi-domain perspective.* The Leadership Quarterly, 1995. **6**(2): p. 219-247.

CHAPTER 12

Social Capital

"Individuals with few weak ties will be deprived of information from distant parts of the social system and will be confined to the provincial news and views of their close friends."[1]

—Mark Granovetter

We humans purposefully seek social connections; indeed, collaboration is essential for our survival. When we connect with others, we do so through a *social object*. A social object, a term coined by Jyri Engestrom, serial social media entrepreneur, is the reason two people engage in communication.[2] For example, if you and a friend play disc golf every Saturday, disc golf is the social object. Examining the social objects in our various relationships can tell us a lot about the diversity of those relationships. In the diagram below, we can see the diversity in social objects, suggesting that the collection of relationships is likely diverse as well. If all three were based on the same social object, the set of relationships would likely be redundant.

When we consider all our relationships, paired with the access to others who we may not already have met, we are referring to our *social capital*. While the term social capital has been around for nearly a century, it has only recently become popular as an area of study within organizational research. It is typically viewed as a resource that provides individuals with strong social contacts and the trust they need in order to effectively work with others. It is even considered as being essential to success.

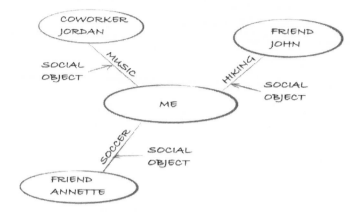

Figure 21: Social Objects

Though not necessarily explicitly communicated, expectations of reciprocation, calculations of trust, and rewards and sanctions attendant to norms, are all central components of social capital and essential to human social existence. Social capital is essentially the connectivity an individual has with other individuals and groups. The result is a resource that individuals obtain from knowing others, and a social identity that comes with being associated with those others.

From a social capital perspective, virtually all relationships have value that can be accumulated and leveraged by individuals. Consider the diagram above. I have three primaries in this network or role-set. Let's classify them as co-workers. If all of the social objects were the same, there is a good chance my co-workers would all have relationship with each other as well and that we would know many of the same people. This would create a high level of *redundancy* in the network. In other words, we all run in the same circles. Considering this from a social capital perspective, if I have high redundancy, then I am not needed as a *broker* in connecting Jordan with Annette. But in this example, the variety in my social objects has created a healthy *non-redundancy* in this network and opportunity for reciprocal exchange. I now have the ability to broker connections, which sets up reciprocal exchange opportunities. Through my three primary members, I have access to nine additional people. Likewise, I can broker connections between my primaries and their networks. For instance, Person A can go through Jordan to get to me, or I can connect Annette with John, or even Person E through John. This is a source of capital and is referred to as *bridging*.

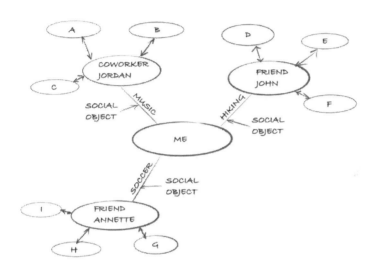

Figure 22: Bridging Social Capital

Primarily based on the work of Ron Burt, this bridging perspective of social capital values the linkages, direct and indirect, in the actor's social relations.[3] From this perspective, social capital is a result of an individual's embeddedness within a network. This suggests that social capital is different from other types of capital in that it cannot be bought, sold, or traded and exists only through the informal networks in which favors are exchanged. The benefits of social capital come in the form of social influence that requires opportunity, motive, and ability to be leveraged. An individual who acts as a bridge between two or more closely connected groups of people potentially gains reciprocal advantages. These people are in the position to span the gap between two distinct groups, thereby allowing them to broker valuable information from one group to another. When we consider this from the perspective of the communications model, these bridgers become the sole encoders and decoders between two otherwise disparate groups.

While an individual's role-set at work may be primarily comprised of co-workers, subordinates, supervisors, etc., it may also include a few folks not from the immediate work setting – like the person that repairs the copier, the UPS delivery person, or even customers or suppliers. The primary idea here is that as social capital, the connections serve as real collateral to the extent that some level of trust exists within the relationships. Trust, then, is a direct measure of the utility of social capital that can be leveraged. In other words, when leveraging the collateral of a friendship, its value equals the amount of trust inherent in that friendship. The social guaranty that is leveraged, and acts as social collateral, has real value because to default (through bad behavior), and bring a negative consequence to the guarantor, is to risk the underlying friendship.

Social capital is considered the "the goodwill available to individuals or groups" that results from the norm of reciprocity within social relationships.[4] As such, social capital can be viewed as an asset that results from a positive social interaction or as relational credits that can be spent. Individuals accrue these credits as a result of the social interactions in the development and maintenance of informal relationships. These credits are idiosyncratic in that they are an asset associated with and unique to the individual, and they function to provide sufficient capital for that individual to leverage as influence. The key tenet of social capital theory is that interpersonal networks are a valuable resource in that the relationships represent a line-of-credit within and between role networks. Essentially, social capital is a personal resource that can be accumulated through social interactions and saved for future use.

The primary idea here is that in general, network connections serve as real collateral, and the level of trust within the relationship defines the extent of that collateral. In other words, when leveraging the collateral of a friendship, its value equals the amount of trust inherent in that friendship. The guaranty is in the notion that the friendship is leveraged social capital and, as collateral, the friendship would be lost on default.

To contrast social capital with human capital, the latter is based on the increased worth or value individuals have based on their acquired knowledge, skills, and abilities, and other characteristics (KSAOs). These KSAOs are represented through credentials such as educational degrees or training programs, as well as job knowledge and experience. Essentially, human capital is the knowledge and skill that an individual has that is the direct result of their investments in education and training. As such, human capital represents a measure of expertness and trustworthiness within a given context, whereas social capital represents a degree of trustworthiness or personal reliability in the eyes of others.

Another often-cited sociologist, Mark Granovetter, suggested that the relationships that comprise our social capital are interpersonal ties that have varying degrees of "embeddedness," and that embedded relations involve repeated interactions over time and are characterized by mutual cooperation and trust.[1] In embedded relationships reciprocity (*exchange*) is at the core, in that people tend to influence – and in turn are influenced by – those with whom they have direct interaction.

Granovetter used the terms *strong ties* (someone you know well), and *weak ties* (a more casual acquaintance) to characterize social capital relationships. Recall from the discussion on relationships that one of the necessary conditions was the expectation of social exchange. He argued that weak ties are the greater resource considering exchange opportunities because they are diffused and as such can reach a larger number of people and travel a greater social distance. This means that weak ties, or casual acquaintances, can be the source of crucial information or influence.

Taking a somewhat sterile and rational perspective, consider for a moment the utility of strong ties versus weak ties. Assuming strong ties require much more time and energy to maintain than weak ties do, and yet weak ties generate more social capital, it stands to reason that weak ties deliver greater social return on investment.

That sterile calculus aside, the central thesis of social capital theory is that *relationships matter* and that social networks are a valuable asset. It is through social interaction that community is constructed, and through community people commit themselves to each other for a common outcome based on trust. It is the very essence of human social life. Trust between individuals in a community provides the bridge to create trust between strangers, or trust by proxy.

Researchers interested in studying social capital have examined the characteristics of the various social networks that people belong to. They differentiated the extent to which these networks were based on informal social activities, or due to memberships in formal groups and organizations. Based on these network characteristics, Michael Woolcock suggested that there are three distinct types of social capital which he labeled as *bonding, bridging,* and *linking.*[5]

Woolcock described *bonding social capital* as a "glue" that ties people in similar situations together. Similar to Granovetter's strong ties, Woolcock suggested that bonding social capital consists of connections such as family members, close friends and neighbors. Bonding social capital refers to those network connections that link people with a strong common feature such as common interests, mutual attraction, or a long or significant history of interaction. Bonding social capital typically consists of immediate family, close friends, and neighbors. There are two types of bonding social capital: *advisors* – those who give advice or psychological support; and *supporters* – those who provide useful information. Regardless, bonding capital tends to reinforce exclusive identities and homogeneous groups. The benefits that bonding capital results in are typically viewed in the form of the personal support.

Bridging social capital, by contrast, is more of a conduit that facilitates connections. It encompasses more distant ties with people who have shared interests, such as loose friendships, coworkers, and acquaintances. Bridging connections are those that link different people through social groups and organizations. These relationships typically consist of more casual relationships based on common interest encounters. There are two types of bridging social capital: *influencers* – those connections that provide access to opportunities or resources; and *connectors* – those people who would be willing to endorse you to others (and in doing so, become purveyors of your reputation). Bridging capital is more inclusive and outward-looking than bonding capital, encompassing people across different social divides. The benefits of bridging capital are realized in coordination, coalition building, and advancement.

Finally, *linking social capital*, which has a latent nature, allows for otherwise people unknown to one another and in dissimilar situations to connect. Linking social capital is considered latent in that it represents what is possible, not what is, and it is based on a myriad of variables that include bonding and bridging relationships, but also reputation, status, and credibility. The benefits of linking social capital are realized when championing new initiatives or implementing change. Simply put, the distinction between bonding, bridging, and linking is that bonding comes from connections between similar individuals, bridging from between those who are diverse, and linking from all those that are not grouped in the previous two, but are immediately possible. Regardless of their differences, the three types of social capital operate together to be a significant resource.

In their book, *In Good Company: How Social Capital Makes Organizations Work* (2001), Don Cohen and Laurence Prusak, demonstrated that higher social capital (in all forms) led to returns such as greater knowledge transfer enabled by established trust relationships, common frames of reference, shared goals, lower transaction costs, higher levels of relational trust and cooperation, lower turnover rates, and greater performance due to organizational stability and shared understanding.[6] They also argued that social capital is an essential element of organizational life, so much so that without it cooperative action isn't possible.

Developing social capital by increasing participation in social networks enables people to build communities, to commit themselves to each other, and to knit the social fabric. To develop social capital, individuals must be proactive and strategic. Social networking is not a passive activity. In order to create solid relationships which support career aspirations, individuals must be prepared to assist others because, at its core, social capital relies on reciprocity.

However, building social capital isn't just beneficial to those just getting started in their careers, in fact, its value actually increases throughout a career. It can be compared to financial investing in that the power of compounding creates a value greater than the investment and results in greater value over time. We can call this a "return on social investment" or ROSI.

To maximize ROSI, relationships must be established initially based on a social object, then nurtured to one based on trust and reciprocity. Once established, they need to be actively maintained, even the loose ties, in order to be effective and valuable. To continuously improve ROSI, it is important to deepen these relationships by staying in touch with your contacts and following up on any opportunities you come across. Considering reciprocity, it is also important to make regular use of these connections by asking for assistance when you need it and by being quick to offer your assistance when others need it. The goal is to establish as much relational trust as possible and that can only develop through interaction. Even though the principle of reciprocity suggests social bank accounts, like financial bank accounts, it is best not to pay too close attention to balances. That could come across as calculative and transactional. Rather take a long-term view and think of it more like social karma.

Karma is defined as "the force generated by a person's actions... [that] determine[s] the nature of the person's next existence."[7] A bona fide leader is not keeping score, a bona fide leader is investing in social capital now with the full belief that when needed it can be called upon. Social capital, similar to reputation, exists beyond the known social landscape and is both known and tangible as well as unknown and intangible. Leaders adopting a social karma perspective are grounded in making the right choices for the right reasons. They emphasize the dignified and respectful treatment of others and have faith that the norm of reciprocity and mutual respect will pay dividends beyond their investments.

Mr. Start-up

Eric had been a bit apprehensive about the move. He wasn't even sure what he was going to do in the new city. His spouse had accepted a position as the head of a major department in a growing mid-sized company. It was too great an opportunity for her to pass up, and he was in a job that was going nowhere, so he supported the change.

He had done some basic research on the city and wanted to try his hand in the non-profit sector there. As soon as they settled in their new house and his wife started her new position, Eric decided to start reaching out to key folks in the new town. He reached out to non-profits across the town, met with their directors, attended their events, and volunteered in their programs. He found himself gravitating to organizations that assisted entrepreneurs in launching new ventures. He was soon a mainstay at various pitch competitions, hack-a-thons, and entrepreneur-related events. As a former collegiate soccer player, he also volunteered to assist the local soccer club, and was quickly recruited to be an assistant coach for a team.

One of the parents on his soccer team, who he knew pretty well because they both served as officers in their local homeowners' association, was good friends with a well-known and very successful local businessman who was raising capital to fund a new small business incubator. The parent brokered an introduction and Eric met the man for coffee. What was supposed to be a 30-minute meeting lasted for over two hours as the two shared ideas and passions and compared notes on who they knew in common and who was doing what. They were interrupted at least five or six times during their meeting by someone stopping to say hello to one or the other.

Six months later, as Eric was sitting in the new entrepreneurship incubator he was running, looking at his picture in the newspaper with the caption "Mr. Startup!" he reflected on the whirlwind of social karma that that brought him to this point.

Reflections

Based on this story, how would you assess Eric's bonding capital?

What about his bridging capital?

What was the social object that connected him with the parent of the soccer player?

What was the social object that connected him with the businessman?

How did the relationship between the soccer parent and the businessman facilitate Eric's opportunities?

What was the risk to the parent in brokering the introduction?

How would you assess the value of Eric "being seen" with the businessman.

How diverse would you guess Eric's network is in this town?

What do you predict Eric's social capital will look like in six more months?

References

1. Mark, G., *Economic Action and Social Structure: The Problem of Embeddedness.* American Journal of Sociology, 1985. **91**(3): p. 481-510.

2. Engestrom, J., *"Why Some Social Network Services Work and Others Don't – Or: The Case for Object-centered Sociality." Zengestrom. April 13. .* 2005.

3. Burt, R.S., *Structural holes.* 2. print. ed. 1995, Cambridge, Mass. [u.a.]: Harvard Univ. Press.

4. Paul, S.A. and K. Seok-Woo, *Social Capital: Prospects for a New Concept.* The Academy of Management Review, 2002. **27**(1): p. 17.

5. Woolcock, M. and D. Narayan, *Social Capital: Implications for Development Theory, Research, and Policy.* The World Bank Research Observer, 2000. **15**(2): p. 225.

6. Cohen, D. and L. Prusak, *In good company.* 1. publ. ed. 2001, Boston, Mass: Harvard Business School Pr.

7. *Merriam-Webster Dictionary.* [cited 2019 Web Page]; Available from: https://www.merriam-webster.com/.

CHAPTER 13

Persuasion

"Thaw with his gentle persuasion is more powerful than Thor with his hammer. The one melts, the other but breaks in pieces."

—Henry David Thoreau [1]

As discussed in Chapter 1, symbolism and the use of symbols in communication is a uniquely human enterprise. If our ability to communicate is a highly sophisticated skill, then consider that persuasion is arguably the highest form of communication. Such a proposition would suggest that the best communicators among us are also our best persuaders. Persuasion is communication with the *intent* of changing a person's or group's ideas, beliefs, or attitudes.[2] Ultimately the goal is to influence that person's behavior as it pertains to an event, idea, object, or another person or group. Within this communication, differing and deliberate approaches are used based on who is being persuaded and about what. Consider again the basic model of all communication: Sender-Message-Channel-Receiver. Within this model the message consists of various symbols understood by both the sender and receiver, yet encoded by the sender and decoded by the receiver. From this perspective, persuasion can be viewed as the deliberate encoding of a message with the intent of it being decoded in such a way as to influence the receiver.

It is not uncommon that we find ourselves in situations where we are trying to persuade another person, but have no existing trust to leverage. These situations call for establishing *swift trust*. To establish swift trust the persuader should focus on several aspects of the social exchange. First, they should find common ground between themselves and the target. This will enhance *identification-based trust*. Second, they should find a way to portray some sense of inter-dependence. This will work to establish *interactional trust* by creating a sense of mutual need. Third, a gentle sense of urgency is needed to reduce opportunity for calculations and perhaps the introduction of a *transactional trust* mechanism. Finally, suggestions to focus on the task-at-hand, rather than the players present, can help to mitigate elements of distrust which may be present.

Aristotle, perhaps the most noted persuader, wrote *Rhetoric* in the 4th century BCE, which included three main rhetorical appeals that are still taught in college writing classes today: *ethos, logos*, and *pathos*.[3] Aristotle suggested that *ethos* is essentially the credibility of the communicator, that *logos* relies on rational appeal in the message itself, and that *pathos* is an appeal to the emotions of the target. His point was that each of these are fundamental to effective persuasion and that while they may vary with each persuasion, some combination of the three is always present in effective persuasion.

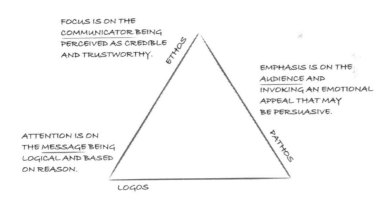

Figure 23: Persuasion

To use *ethos,* the persuader must present an image that is credible or trustworthy. For the persuader this means they must get the target to trust them, their credentials, or even their motives for the persuasion to be effective. Remember the types of trust? Transactional, interactional, relational, identificational, intuitional (and let's add reputational) may all be leveraged by the influencer as the foundation of an ethos-based persuasion. For the persuader's argument to be effective, the persuader must present themselves as credible or knowledgeable on the topic.

Credibility is a variation on identificational trust and reputational trust. Credibility can be conferred through recognized expertise such as a diploma or certification. It can also be conferred through reputation, such as being widely regarded as an expert on the subject. Self-presentation or impression management can be effectively used by the persuader to "present" a credible image. How we dress, speak, and conduct ourselves all contribute to the image that others hold of us. Consider the investment banker wearing dark sunglasses, blue jeans, and sandals trying to convince you to switch your investment portfolio to his firm. He must play the role that we imagine of an investment banker. To the extent he matches our pre-conceived expectations (think confirmation bias), we afford him some degree of credibility.

Logos appeals to the target's sense of logic, in that it is a calculation of whether the persuader is presenting a compelling argument. This goes back to how we make sense and how we know. Since logos is an appeal to logic, it is often accompanied by the use of facts and figures that support the influencer's position. It can enhance the influencer's ethos by making them appear to be a credible expert. However, perceived misuse of information can quickly erode credibility and even undermine trust. In the absence of using data and information, the influencer may have to rely on reason. Reason appeals to widely held truths or "generic sense" and calls upon the persuader to connect that sense and appeal to the target's sense of reason instead of empirically supported logic.

Lastly, *pathos* is an appeal to the emotions of the target or audience. For the most effective persuasion, use of ordinary evidence will not do. The most effective persuaders present evidence in a passionate manner. They use stories and descriptive language in a way that supplements their empirical data with anecdotes, metaphors, and analogies to reduce sterility and add realism to their positions. The creative use of language and symbolism paints a visual image and adds an emotional and human element to the persuader's point of view. Listeners tend to absorb information in proportion to its vividness.

Pathos invokes the use of symbolism in the form of metaphors, simile, imagery, or passionate pleas. The persuader is not appealing to the rational side of the target, rather the deep-rooted and emotional sense that often lurks beneath the surface. Pathos can overpower ethos and logos if used well. Ask any salesperson what form of persuasion is dominant in consumer decisions and they'll likely tell you it is the buyer's emotions that win. When coupled with logos, it can be a one-two punch.

As mentioned before, symbolism can be used to great effect to support pathos-based influence when aimed at a carefully chosen target audience. Consider that beer and truck commercials regularly appeal to the emotions of the middle-class sports fan during televised professional sports, whereas the underprivileged child, with a dramatic teardrop on their cheek, is more likely to appear during a commercial break of a daytime talk show or evening drama.

Good persuaders are aware of the primacy of emotions and have a strong and accurate sense of their audience's emotional state. They are empathetic. This requires tremendous investments in social interaction. Seemingly innocuous interactions (chatting at the copier, lunchtime banter, chit-chat in the hall) are all opportunities to gather information regarding the emotional issues that others might have.

Combining any two of the three elements (ethos, logos, pathos) can enhance the persuaders influence attempt and perhaps overpower a deficiency in the third. Recall what the Milgram studies and the Stanford prison experiments revealed – they both demonstrated how good people can be transformed into perpetrators of evil, and how healthy people can begin to experience pathological reactions as a result of situational forces, i.e. a combination of ethos and pathos. Both were impactful demonstrations of the power inherent in the situation to influence individual attitudes, values, and behavior.

Indeed, Milgram suggested that certain conditions needed to be present to persuade the subject to act in a manner that they would not otherwise act in.[4] He suggested that some form of logical justification (logos) needed to be present. In the case of his experiments, it was that it was an "important study," it was "science." He also appealed to ethos by having a "scientist" dress in a lab-coat and hold a clipboard as though he was an "expert" while remaining in close proximity to the subject. Finally, he reduced the likelihood of an emotional (pathos) resistance by removing the subject from direct proximity to the person being "shocked" and labeling (dehumanizing) them as "learners."

Finally, the Milgram experiment demonstrated that obedience to authority is valued behavior (ethos) in our culture. Most of us assume that obedience to authority is a civic virtue and we rarely consider that such authority could be dangerous. We learned this as children. We were taught to obey persons in positions of authority from our first forays into independent behavior. Arguably, the very essence of human societies is predicated on the principal of obedience.

Perhaps the most noted expert on what it means to influence is Robert Cialdini. He calls his research "The Science of Persuasion" and suggests that there are six principles of persuasion that get others to say yes to an influencer's requests.[5] He suggested that these persuasion tactics are tools to subtly guide human behavior. The six principles – *reciprocity, scarcity, authority, consistency, liking,* and *consensus* – serve as satisficing mechanisms in our cognitive processing. Cialdini suggests that in contemporary times our cognitive processes are increasingly overloaded, and as such we need shortcuts for decision-making more than ever. This suggests that understanding the principles of persuasion may have never been more relevant. According to Cialdini, understanding how principles work and, more importantly, using them in an ethical manner, can significantly increase the chances that someone will be influenced by your persuasion effort. Interestingly, each of Cialdini's principles fits neatly into Aristotle's ideas on persuasion using ethos, logos, and pathos.

The first of Cialdini's principles, *reciprocity*, has already been discussed in Chapter 7. To revisit, the norm of *reciprocity* or social exchange can produce a sense of indebtedness, which can be a powerful tool in persuasion. As we perceive a sense of indebtedness to another, the act of allowing ourselves to become "persuaded" becomes a currency in our debt repayment or deposit. An interesting point about leveraging this tactic is that it works best when the influencer is the first to give and does so in a way that is personalized and unexpected. It seems that an unexpected and personalized touch on a favor or gesture is valued higher in the "accounting" process. From this perspective we can see that reciprocity is an emotional phenomenon, and can thereby be primarily categorized as pathos, but interestingly it can also be viewed as a logical calculus, which could also categorize it as logos.

Scarcity is a powerful persuasive approach that plays on a fundamental human instinct to secure, protect, and conserve resources. Essentially, when something is perceived as having limited availability, we assign more value to it. We are thereby persuaded to desire it more. Effective persuaders not only tell people about the benefits they'll gain in making a certain decision, but also what they stand to lose if they if they do not. Similar to reciprocity, we can see that scarcity is an emotional perception, and thereby can also be categorized as pathos.

Authority is similar to identification-based trust and our previous discussions on self-presentation. We buy into an authority figure's presentation of expertness or knowing. We tend to satisfice when the expert shares information by accepting it as truth (authority method). Consider the example of the Milgram experiment – in this study, subjects were more likely to be persuaded to inflict pain upon others when an authority figure was present. We know that our self-presentation can make us appear to be a credible, knowledgeable authority, and we also know that the best presentations illicit the help of supporting actors which give credibility to our performance. Following this understanding, we can easily put this under ethos even though our assessment may have been influenced by perceptions and symbolism.

Consistency is a powerful force in persuasion because it is the basis of interactional and relational trust. Additionally, consistency is the basis of reputation formation, which is a substitute for direct trust. Both trust and reputation provide a valuable satisficing shortcut in conditions of uncertainty, thereby facilitating persuasion. Additionally, consistency leverages the tendency that most of us have to be consistent in our own behavior. So, small initial commitments can serve as the base for larger more significant commitments, simply because of the validation from the consistency between the two. Consistency can be categorized as ethos even though our calculus may have been cut short by satisficing.

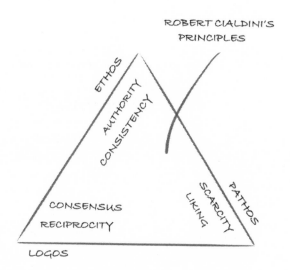

Figure 24: Principles of Persuasion

The notion of *liking* also relates to trust in that we are invoking identificational trust. The two primary contributing factors to liking are physical attractiveness (think symbolism and self-presentation) and similarity (identificational trust). With both attractiveness and similarity, we are more likely to be receptive to persuasion. Finally, we like people who pay us compliments, people who cause a positive emotional feeling.

We feel as though these people really have empathy for us, know who we are and understand what our talents are. The more we like someone, the more we are open to their persuasion attempts. Liking is easy to categorize as pathos, as we certainly identify with those we like.

Finally, *consensus* is essentially the social forces at play in sensemaking. Essentially, consensus is most effective when in conditions of uncertainty or ambiguity (i.e. when we need to make sense). When we are uncertain (our intra-subjective sense), we look to the other levels of sensemaking to inform us and to help us make sense. This points back to logos in that we seek confirmation from others. Consensus is a form of logic in that it represents unified position or thought. Consider the "eight out of ten dentists choose…" statement used in toothpaste advertising. Our minds process the logic as "it must be good if eight out of ten recommend it."

A discussion on persuasion would be incomplete without taking a look at the darker side. Commonly referred to as Machiavellianism, this form of persuasion received its name based on the writings of the sixteenth-century philosopher Niccolò Machiavelli and his masterpiece *The Prince*.[6] The Machiavellian approach is perhaps best captured in the book *The 48 Laws of Power* by Robert Greene. This approach employs the tools of manipulation and deceit to persuade others, and central to this manipulation is the notion of "indirectness." In the book's preface, Greene wrote:

> The successful courtier learned over time to make all of his moves indirect; if he stabbed an opponent in the back, it was with a velvet glove and the sweetest of smiles on his face… the perfect courtier got his way through seduction, charm, deception, and subtle strategy, always planning several moves ahead. Life in the court was a never-ending game that required constant vigilance and tactical thinking. It was civilized war.[7]

Using soft strategies such as persuasion, versus hard tactics like power, bona fide leaders allow for their followers to become wiser, freer, more autonomous, and more likely to think critically. This is the aim of *servant leadership*, a term coined in 1970 by Robert Greenleaf.[8] Servant leadership is a contemporary leadership philosophy that emphasizes serving over leading. With servant leadership the focus is on serving the needs of others first. It involves having respect for others' perspectives, providing support to meet their goals, involving them in important conversations and decisions, and creating a sense of belonging where members take care of each other. Persuasion is essential to servant leadership as the servant-leader sells ideas more than declares them. Effective persuasion also places a high premium on understanding others' emotions, personalities, and other idiosyncrasies. Thoughtful leaders allow followers to make choices. A bona fide leader persuades as much as they direct.

Death of a Sale

The customer was excited. He had done his homework and had nearly convinced himself that the high-end luxury car was going to be his choice for a new vehicle. He could afford it; that was not the issue, instead he needed to be convinced that the luxury was justified and resale value justified the expense. He brought along his wife and child with him for the final decision. As he drove in the lot, he could see the team of salespeople just inside the showroom He had been through this before; they were assessing him and the vehicle he was currently driving. They were already making assumptions about his income level and his motivation for coming to the lot.

After a few short exchanges, one of them moved towards the door to step outside. The customer wondered if this salesman considered himself "lucky" or "unlucky" for having to approach the small family that drove up in a nine-year-old minivan. He guessed the latter.

As the salesman introduced himself, the customer explained that they were looking for a new vehicle and had read the reviews on the luxury vehicle and that it was on their shortlist. The customer just wanted to drive the car and experience the quality difference that would justify the price. As he and his wife and daughter drove away for a test drive, he was instantly impressed with the vehicle's performance and feel. He had noticed the vehicle's well-known logo and was excited to think he would finally own one. The leather interior was spacious, stylish, and comfortable. The car handled exceptionally well and had plenty of power. The customer was mostly convinced and he could tell his wife and daughter liked the vehicle as well. It was mostly going to come down to negotiating a price he thought was fair.

As they returned to the lot, once again the salespeople were standing together and sharing short exchanges. The customer knew that he was the likely topic. Their salesman moved to the door, putting a paternalistic smile on his face. He approached the family and asked the perfunctory questions: "So what'd you think? How was it?" and "How did you like how it handled?" As he asked the questions, his eyes darted back and forth from the husband to the wife to the daughter as if he were trying to gauge their interest in the car.

His eyes settled on the young girl as he began to espouse the safety features of the vehicle. He asked the young girl if she felt safe in that car. He went on to say how much safer it was than lesser-priced vehicles and that recently one of those cheaper vehicles had been in an accident and that it was "cut in half" by a pick-up truck that hit it broadside.

As the customer drove away, he tore up the salesman's business card. The salesman had aggravated him so much that he couldn't stand the thought of buying a vehicle from him. The family went to another dealership that carried a more modest line of cars, and after learning of the virtues and price of a particular model, they purchased it on the spot. In the following few weeks, the luxury salesman's calls were not returned and his emails were deleted.

Reflections

What assumptions did the salesman make?

What symbolism was present?

What persuasive approach did the salesman use?

What approach should he have used?

How did the salesman undermine his own credibility?

How did the salesman attempt to use Cialdini's persuasion tools?

Was a Machiavellian tactic used?

References

1. Thoreau, H.D., *Walden : And, On the Duty of Civil Disobedience*. 2008, [Waiheke Island]: The Floating Press.
2. *Leadership: Theory and Practice, 8th Edition*. 2018, Ringgold, Inc.
3. Aristotle and C.D.C. Reeve, *Rhetoric*. 2018, Hackett Publishing Company, Inc: Indianapolis ; Cambridge.
4. Milgram, S., *Behavioral Study of obedience*. The Journal of Abnormal and Social Psychology, 1963(4): p. 371.
5. Cialdini, R.B., *Influence*. Rev. ed., 1. Collins business essentials ed. ed. 2007, New York: Collins.
6. Machiavelli, N., *Theœ prince*. Theœ modern library of the world's best books. Vol. 49. 1940, New York: The moderne library.
7. Greene, R., *The 48 Laws Of Power*. The Robert Greene Collection. 2010, London: Profile Books.
8. Greenleaf, R.K., *The servant as leader*. 1970: Center for Applied Studies.

CHAPTER 14

Social Power

"Power is used to take action, and one way to determine who has power is to observe who benefits, and to what extent, from organizational actions, particularly decisions or actions that are contested."

—Jeffrey Pfeffer [1]

"Man's flight through life is sustained by the power of his knowledge."

—Austin 'Dusty' Miller, quote on the Eagle & Fledgling statue at the U.S. Air Force Academy

For this chapter we should rearrange Miller's quote to read, "Man's flight through life is sustained by the knowledge of his power." Unlike persuasion which uses indirect methods to influence others, *social power* is the ability to influence or change the behavioral outcome of another person by leveraging certain tools or attributes. Volumes have been written on the topic of social power and there are many variations on the types of social power. Most definitions of power describe it as a possession that is held and available for discretionary use. For example, Merriam-Webster defines it as a "possession of control, authority, or influence over others."[2] Almost all available definitions follow the same basic premise, that power is a possession held by one and used to influence another. We tend to view someone who has power over us, or has the power to influence us, as though they "possess" this capability, but what if they didn't?

Social power differs from social influence, in that social power is an ability which may or may not be used, whereas social influence is an effect. So then social power is a source of influence and authority that one person has over another or others. Where does a person get this power from? In short, social power is determined and defined by the needs and wants of those others. It is, at its essence, a dependency. A dependency that exists and is fueled by a perception that the path to satisfying that need or want must go through someone else.

When considering sources of personal power, it is useful to consider what motivates us to act. We have already discussed expectancy theory as a motivator for managing impressions, but for this discussion we will turn to a more fundamental theory on human motivation.

One of the first ideas on what motivates people to action was suggested by Abraham Maslow. Maslow suggested that we are motivated to act based on a hierarchy of needs.[3] Maslow arranged these needs from the basic need for existence (*physiological*), to a need for *safety*, to social needs such as *belonging* and *esteem*, to the highest need for personal accomplishment (*self-actualization*). He argued that we all are motivated to satisfy these needs and that if we can understand these needs in others, we have the keys to unlock motivation in others. He also argued that these needs were hierarchical in that we would not be motivated to satisfy a higher-level need until a lower one is satisfied. Maslow called this necessary hierarchy *prepotency*.

Maslow's widely popular perspective is useful in introducing the notion that power is connected to needs, yet the issue of prepotency is problematic and constraining. Clayton Alderfer, a noted psychologist, further developed Maslow's hierarchy of needs by collapsing the hierarchy into three broad categories of needs (*existence*, *relatedness* and *growth*), known as ERG theory.[4] Alderfer also suggested they do not need to be arranged in a hierarchy, meaning that basic needs can exist at the same time as a social need. For this discussion on power, we will borrow from ERG theory and categorize needs as *basic, social*, and *esteem*. We will also drop the idea of prepotency, and suggest that a need creates the opportunity for a dependency.

We examine these dependencies as *needs* not *wants* because wants can be turned on and off. We may want something badly, but it is not an imperative to our well-being to get it. Wants thereby make for fleeting and temporary dependencies, as our desires change, or some new want supplants the previous one and the temporary dependency evaporates. Wants then, are something that we desire and yet do not have. Unlike needs, which are limited in nature, non-discretionary, and do not change over time, wants are unlimited in nature, discretionary, and constantly changing. A want emerges due to a lack or shortage of something desired and fades with acquisition or the emergence of a stronger want. Wants can also be described as those desires that can be satisfied by an object, service, or activity. Since most of us have limited resources, we cannot have all of the goods, services, or activities we want, and as a result we must choose which wants to pursue and which ones not to pursue. Economists call this opportunity cost.

Human needs (which are limited in nature, non-discretionary, do not change over time) can be grouped into two categories: *physiological* and *psychological*. Physiological needs are those that meet the demands of our physical self, such as the essentials of life – food, water, oxygen. Physiological needs also include those things necessary to sustain the physical self over time such as shelter, sleep, freedom from injury, and even physical contact. Psychological needs are those needs essential to the cognitive self, such as autonomy, competency, and relatedness to others. These essentials of social existence also include self-esteem and achievement. When we combine physiological needs with psychological needs, we arrive back at the three broad categories: basic, social, and esteem.

Basic needs are those necessary to sustain the physical self, *social needs* are those that connect us with others, and *esteem needs* fulfill our need for achievement and a sense of worth. What is interesting about needs is that one cannot act as a substitute for another, nor are they optional. In other words, extra food or oxygen will not substitute for a lack of water. Excess of autonomy cannot compensate for a lack of competency. All other desires are discretionary wants, or they represent some surrogate or temporary solution for an actual need.

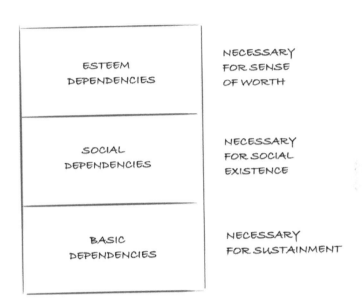

Figure 25: Needs Theory of Motivation

Now before we can consider social power, let's categorize our needs and wants into types of dependencies. A *dependency* exists when a need cannot be met by an individual and so they must rely on another to satisfy the need. We can categorize dependencies consistent with the needs categories of basic, social, and esteem.

Basic dependencies are those that we rely on for our physical sustainment. They can include the source of our income, or the capacity of that income to make a house payment or fix a car. We may rely on them for our need for safety and sustenance, both for ourselves and for our families. *Social dependencies* represent our longing to belong to some social entity greater than ourselves; it is our need for friendship and community. Social dependencies can range from a yearning for companionship to a desire to be a member of a certain team or group. Finally, *esteem dependencies* are those that lead to success as we have defined it. It might mean getting selected for a big promotion, it might be the achievement of some lofty goal such as a graduate degree, or it might be some physical achievement such as running a marathon. Regardless, achievement dependencies represent those things or people that are critical to our success.

Many of the dependencies we perceive in our lives stem from wants and are exaggerated. With a little mental effort we can choose to re-punctuate them, find substitutes for them, or neutralize them, thereby freeing and empowering ourselves.

Re-punctuation involves changing how we think about the dependency. To re-punctuate a dependency, we have to mentally "re-define" the need. Consider the dependency on employment – if I could somehow re-define how I might survive without my current job (or the degree to which my continued employment is linked to my boss), I would then re-define the primacy of my dependency on my boss.

The use of substitutes involves shifting the dependency from one individual to another. If I am dependent on a particular relationship in order to be included with the lunch crowd at work, I may have a social dependency. But if I can find a different group to go to lunch with, my social need will be met by that group and the dependency on the first individual will be weakened. I have found a substitute for that social dependency.

Finally, to neutralize a dependency we seek to remove it altogether. One manifestation of this is to become fatalistic. Once we resign ourselves to a certain outcome, the intensity of the dependency fades and perhaps vanishes altogether. Consider the dependencies that exist when hoping for a significant promotion. We can be so reliant upon key individuals for our success. Once we feel (whether it is accurate or not) we are no longer in the running, those dependencies suddenly disappear.

To better understand the dependency perspective of power, we will follow convention with the notable study of power conducted by social psychologists John R. P. French and Bertram Raven in 1959.[5] They divided power into five separate and distinct forms and suggested that the basic types of power include: *reward power, coercive power, expert power, legitimate power*, and *referent power*. We will add two more to that list – *information power* and *connection power*.

French and Raven defined reward power as the control one has over valued resources. Coercive power refers to the ability to inflict punishment, even physical punishment. Expert power is the perception that another has superior knowledge. Legitimate power stems from an individual's ability to make decisions that influence others and is typified by rank or position. Referent power refers to those people who others wish to be like or like to be around. All of these types of power can either be categorized as positional or personal.

While the French and Raven bases of power is a widely accepted taxonomy, many have proposed additional types of power, some as many as 14. Most of these additions are merely variations of the original five, but two stand out as somewhat distinct and relevant to contemporary advances in technology and communication. Proposed by Hershey and Blanchard's study[6], information power and connection power have also been widely accepted as distinct sources of power, so we will consider them along with the French and Raven five.

Each of the classic power types are characterized as an ability belonging to the wielder. Coercive power is depicted as the ability to punish; legitimate power is seen as the ability to influence others through some formal position in an organization; reward power is the ability to reward; connection power is the ability to broker relationships and extend networks; information power is the ability to control and restrict information flow; expert power is the ability to control process and progress; referent power is the ability to influence others' liking; information power is having access to valuable and restricted information; and connection power involves controlling access to valuable others. One thing is common across all the types of power: each of these is viewed as an ability or possession.

The "possession" perspective of power is limiting and places the target of power in a defeatist position. To view power as a possession of another is to assume a lack of control in the exchange. To view power as a possession of ourselves is to assume we have more influence than we actually have. Rather than viewing power as a possession, let's consider it as a dependency. The point here is that no power would exist if it were not for a dependency being in place. The power-person cannot control the dependency, they can only satisfy the need; the dependent-person will yield to the power-person as long as they see them as the sole source of their need satisfaction. From this perspective, when we are the dependent-person, we make ourselves an active participant in social exchange. We give power to another. We are not mere passive recipients of another's will, instead we are co-conspirators in the power relationship.

Reward power, a positional-based power, refers to the perception that others have of one's ability to influence the rewards that they desire. These rewards can be bonuses, transfers, raises, promotions, desirable assignments, training opportunities, and even simple compliments. If you are perceived as being in the "decision space" for these desired outcomes, then others will likely view you as having power. Remember expectancy theory here. First, they must believe that some behavior will lead to some outcome, then they must believe they have the capacity to deliver that behavior, and finally, they must desire the outcome. Without expectancy theory, reward power does not work. Also, remember here the tenets of social exchange, as you give rewards, you are either paying back for a job well done (fixing a debit with a deposit) or you are creating a surplus (to use for a future withdrawal).

Coercive power, also a positional-based power, is often viewed as the opposite of reward power, and refers to the perception that someone is in the "decision space" to deny or remove something that is valued by another. The argument can be made (and has been), that the removal of a punishment can be characterized as a reward and that the constructs of reward and coercive power are not necessarily opposite constructs, but rather variations of the same perspective (i.e. the brokering good or bad of desired outcomes). Interestingly, managers often rely heavily on these two forms of power, but the result is often an impoverished social landscape that never rises above the realm of *transactional trust* because the behaviors desired are achieved primarily through the management of transactions.

Expert power, again a positional-based power, is when we perceive that another person has knowledge and skills that are valuable to us or that can help us achieve some desired outcome. In these situations we are likely to grant that person some ability to influence us. Remember here the discussion on self-presentation in that what is important for expert power is that we perceive them as an expert. Recall also the discussion on symbolism – the stethoscope around the neck with the white lab-coat screams expertise to us. Expert power includes: technical knowledge, social knowledge (political skill), tactical knowledge, physical skill, procedural knowledge, tacit knowledge, confidence (self- presentation), decisiveness, *reputation,* and experience among others. It is no wonder that an adage throughout the ages and the meaning behind Miller's quote has been "Knowledge is power!"

Legitimate power, a personal-based power, is power that is resident within a certain role. It implies a high degree of reward, coercive, and even expert power, but it is not limited to just those. This power also includes the ability to set agendas, shape or change our thinking, and even choose the range of awards and sanctions to be used by others. Legitimate power is also "hard-wired" into our psyches (recall the power of childhood experiences). Socially, we are conditioned to respect authority; it is the foundation of human civilization. From this perspective, legitimate power influences our perceptions of social hierarchies, cultural norms, and organizational culture (recall extra-subjective and generic sense).

Interestingly, legitimate power can be fragile. It comes with the position, not the person, so once the person is removed from the position, so goes the power they once wielded. It also exists within a given context or role-set. Consider a CEO that has considerable power (dependencies) in their organization trying to influence a group of teenagers at the mall. They have no dependency on this otherwise powerful CEO, so they would laugh away her commands. Bottom-line, those that rely on legitimate power alone limit the time and scope of their influence to a situational context that might be fleeting and is not transferable across contexts.

Referent power, also a personal-based power, is that ability to influence based on another's liking, affection, trust or identification (recall relational trust, identification-based trust, relationships, persuasion). When we think of famous people (with fame as a construct different from reputation) we can see how they have the power to influence us in many ways, which is why they are valuable assets to marketing everything from what we wear to what we eat and drink. Referent power can be quite potent and easily abused. We are quick to follow those we like and may not be as critical of them when the outcomes are not what we desired. Also, and from a *social exchange* perspective, if the currency of exchange is our perception (self-presentation) that they "like us," then this type of power can be a nearly infinite resource. However, as with all types of social power, someone who wields this power (i.e. is likable), but lacks integrity and honesty, may use it for personal advantage at the expense of others, which over time would make them less likeable and thereby undermine their own power.

Information power is a power that can be categorized as either a personal- or positional-based power depending on whether the information flow is relative to a specific position or instead based on a relationship. From this perspective, information is seen as a valuable resource to be used to achieve some objective. Whether that information is "insider" information based on an informed position, or "grapevine" information based on an individual's network, it can easily be leveraged for influence.

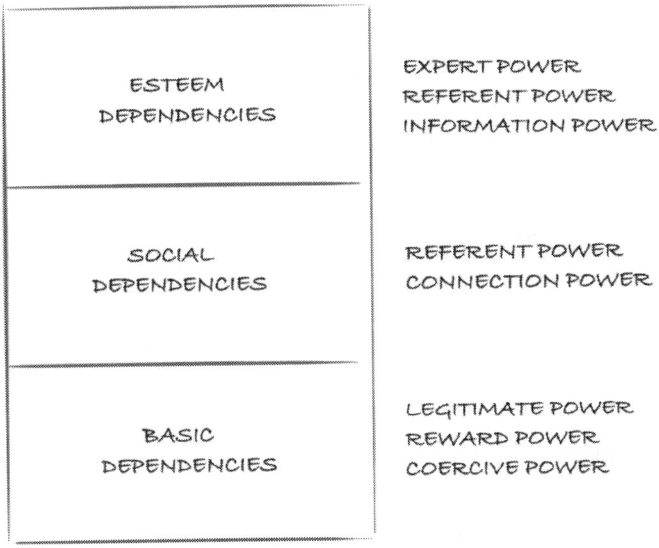

ESTEEM DEPENDENCIES	EXPERT POWER REFERENT POWER INFORMATION POWER
SOCIAL DEPENDENCIES	REFERENT POWER CONNECTION POWER
BASIC DEPENDENCIES	LEGITIMATE POWER REWARD POWER COERCIVE POWER

Figure 26: Types of Social Power

Finally, connection power can also be categorized as personal- or position-based in that the network can be a part of a legitimate organizational structure or based on personal relationships. More commonly referred to as "networking" these days, the power here is the ability to connect two unconnected parties, to be a social broker. Those that need to be connected to another will recognize the connection power of another to broker the connection. This type of power is a central feature in organizational politics and an essential component of political skill.

When we align the various types of power with the categories of dependencies we can see "categories of power" emerge. While every type of power can be leveraged in all needs categories, the chart below suggests where they are most salient. This may be a useful perspective in that if all of the situations where we feel dependent are expert, referent, and information power dynamics, then we could assess that we are most vulnerable in the "esteem" dependencies. With this knowledge, we could begin to envision suitable neutralizers and substitutes to reduce our dependencies on others and thereby limiting their power over us.

With leadership comes power, even with servant leadership. The issue arises with when and how to wield it. Used appropriately and in the right measure, it can enhance a reputation. Knowing when to shift from persuasion to power can be a defining moment for a leader. Equally defining in a negative sense is to use too much power or to use it too soon. Exploiting dependencies is forgoing social exchange and reciprocity and moving straight to coercion. While drastic times call for drastic measures, situations that are less than pressing are better served by persuasion. Bona fide leaders understand this and also can see the dependencies all around them and are sophisticated in their understanding of power dynamics.

The New Guy

Brett was relatively new to the organization and midway through his second month. As a member of an elite department, his office was located in what was called the "bowling alley." It was called this because it was a collection of offices along a hallway that was typically a hotbed of activity. This day was no different, as the sounds and chatter of all of Brett's co-workers who were preparing reports, getting ready for some meeting, or discussing how to best do this or that, seemed constant and in chorus. As Brett began to work on the project, he considered its importance, his dependence on others for their expertise, the consequences of getting it wrong, the potential for his future for getting it right, and overall, his relatively low position in the hierarchy. He focused his mind on the project and soon the cacophony of sound that was so loud before was no longer noticeable as he became engrossed in his work.

He was not sure how long he had been working on the details for the project, but he suddenly noticed the deafening silence. Alarm bells went off in his head. Something was wrong, terribly wrong. He couldn't even hear Steve, who could typically always be heard telling a joke or sharing a laugh. Steve was also the one that seemed to always help him with "insights" as to how things "really got done." He was a real source of information, but more importantly, Steve knew everyone in the building and was well-liked by all. It took a second for Brett to realize that the silence was due to everyone being gone. He was late for a very important event.

It was the former and very popular department head's retirement luncheon. As he rushed to the crowded conference room where the reception was scheduled, he was dismayed to find the door closed. Not wanting to interrupt, he listened for a break in the muffled voices. After ten minutes or so, the moment arrived. He reached to open the door, but it was locked! His attempt at illegal entry did not go unnoticed however, and the door opened. It was former department head, the man loved by everyone. As Brett looked into his eyes, there were tears. As he looked around the room, there was not a dry eye to be seen. He had interrupted the climactic conclusion to the emotional farewell speech.

The room was silent except for the sniffling. Wishing he could crawl under a rock and feeling the unfriendly eyes of the entire department upon him, he made his entrance. As he passed the new department head, he paused to extend his hand and express his apologies for the interruption and tardiness. The new department head turned his back on Brett and refused the handshake. Standing there, hand outstretched, he felt naked; he was thoroughly humiliated, so he slithered in to take a seat in the rear of the room. As he took his seat, Brett quickly glanced around for a sympathetic colleague, yet averting eyes told him that he was alone in his blunder. That is until he looked at Steve. Steve was always telling jokes and had a way of making everyone like him. He seemed to have impeccable timing with his humor and could always reduce the tension with a quip or comment. Steve's eyes seemed to smile at Brett as if to say he understood. Brett felt as though he had found an ally in an otherwise hostile room.

He quickly learned what those eyes were smiling about. He was about to get shot between the eyes with a razor-sharp Steve quip. Steve's sense of humor was not bound by context – he was able to bring humor into the most tense of situations. This was one of those moments. Steve broke the awkward silence in the room with the words: "We're going to have to work on your timing." As the laughter began to erode the tension, Brett realized he had witnessed a master at the top of his game. He also realized that Steve's quip, though at his expense, was also an offering of friendship. The joke signaled to the rest of the department that Brett was one of them, that he was on the team.

On their way out of the room following the conclusion of the ceremony, Steve whispered "Don't worry about it Brett, you just added a chapter to the history of our department, and that is a good thing for you."

Reflections

How are the various types of power evident in this story?

Who has the most power?

Who has the least power?

Did Brett gain power in this situation or lose it?

What dependencies were obvious in this story?

How might Brett work to gain power?

How might neutralizers and substitutes be in Brett's future?

References

1. Pfeffer, J., *Managing with power*. 2. print. ed. 1992, Boston, Mass: Harvard Business School Pr.
2. *Merriam-Webster Dictionary.* [cited 2019 Web Page]; Available from: https://www.merriam-webster.com/.
3. Maslow, A.H., *Some Theoretical Consequences of Basic Need-Gratification.* Journal of personality, 1948. **16**(4): p. 402.
4. Alderfer, C.P., *Existence, relatedness, and growth; human needs in organizational settings.* 1972, Free Press: New York.
5. French, J.R.P. and B. Raven, *The Bases of Social Power*, in *Group Dynamics*, D. Cartwright and A. Zander, Editors. 1959, Harper Row: New York. p. 259-269.
6. Hersey, P., K.H. Blanchard, and W.E. Natemeyer, *Situational Leadership, Perception, and the Impact of Power.* Group & Organization Studies, 1979. **4**(4): p. 418-428.

PART THREE

PERSPECTIVES

In this final section we visit multiple viewpoints and explore what is revealed when we consider situations from different viewpoints. We look at the powerful forces that exist in organizational culture and how we are socialized into those cultures. We take the stage and peek behind the curtain to view social interactions as theatrical performances. Organizational politics is explored and presented as a positive force in organizational social interactions. We visit what it means to be a follower and address the idea that leaders need followers, who in turn need leaders. We consider morals, values, and ethics and their role in how we frame our understanding and decision-making. Finally, in the last chapter, we look at what it means to be a leader.

Being a bona fide leader is more about knowing yourself, knowing others, and accurately *seeing* situations than it is about specific traits, behaviors, or actions. Leadership is a swirling, ever-changing dynamic milieu that defies steps or rules. It is more about the servant-leader answering the call than aspiring for the role. To that point, we are all a perfect leader for some situation, but to be that perfect leader, we must be true to our character, we must be bona fide. If we are focused on trying to be the leader we think we should be, we may very well miss our call.

CHAPTER 15

Cultural Perspective

"Culture is to a group what personality or character is to an individual."

—Edgar Schein[1]

When we examine the culture of an organization that we currently belong to, it can be difficult to be impartial because we are imbedded within it and are a part of it. In order to appreciate the cultural currents that influence us, we must take a meta-perspective or examine them from a "distant perch." In order to recognize these not-so-visible forces that influence our behavior, we need to know what to look for and be able to "take inventory" on the visible aspects of culture such as symbols, stories, rituals and ceremonies, and attitudes and norms.

It is important to differentiate culture from climate, as the latter is often considered the former. The difference between the two is similar to the earlier discussion on traits versus states. *Culture* is like a trait in that it is an enduring, slowly changing core characteristic like a personality. *Climate,* on the other hand, is more like a state. It consists of temporary attitudes, perceptions, and opinions that are usually in response to a specific incident or occurrence, just as with a state. This discussion is on culture not climate. To that end, culture is defined as "a socially constructed attribute of organizations that serves as the social glue binding an organization together."[2]

We can begin by looking and listening for some of the most obvious and tell-tale signs of culture – artifacts. These artifacts can range from physical objects such as furniture or plaques on the wall to nuances of language and jargon. The main point is that they have meaning and that is why they are on display or in use. They are symbolic representations of what is important to the organization. So, the question to start with is "what are the artifacts present in the organization, and what does it mean that they are present?" What hangs on the wall? What is on the wall or on display in prominent locations, such as elevator exits, versus the more obscure, as in down a long hallway? What is present in the executive suite, the meeting room, or the place where the customer visits? How are offices adorned and where are they located?

In addition to the visible aspects of culture, we can also look to the "lore" of the organization. What are the stories that are told and retold? Why are they passed along? These stories may range from being based, largely or loosely, on some actual occurrence and sometimes they may be purely fictional, but they are told and re-told for a reason. They are often the source of the organization's history and passed down from old-timers to new-comers, generation after generation. The stories being told have an underlying meaning or purpose; consider *what it means* that they are being told. What is the relevance of the story?

Stories can serve to connect the past to the present and often provide us with context for how to think about the future. Stories also help us understand the nuances of organizational life. Stories can reveal what is valued and what is not valued by members of the organization. From this perspective it is important to note that no single person or authority controls what stories are told, rather, it is an organic by-product of the culture itself. These stories provide us with our "sense" of ourselves within the organization. Who are the company exemplars? Why are they the exemplars? Do the stories about these exemplars get embellished? If so, what is the embellishment and what does *that* mean?

As mentioned in the chapter on Humor, often the stories are funny. What does it mean that a particular story is funny? Would it be funny to an outsider? Why? Why not? What does it say to us that a particular story only has humor within the context of the organization? Remember that for humor to be present, there must be some shared perspective – humor only is humorous within a given culture or context. The degree to which people find the story funny may well define the breadth of the culture, from the culture of a small work-group to an entire organization.

Another source of information regarding a company's culture, and one that was discussed in the Dramaturgical chapter, are the rituals and ceremonies that permeate the organization. A ritual refers to group of actions performed for their symbolic value. Rituals are also events that are staged with some degree of regularity, such as "Free Lunch First Fridays," or "ring the bell with every sale." The specific purpose of rituals differs according to the culture, but typically they exist to reinforce some value or purpose and can be an individual or group activity.

On the other hand, a ceremony is performed on special occasions. As such, ceremonies are more significant and less regular than rituals. They tend to acknowledge significant achievements, milestones, and rites of passage. The purpose of ceremonies is to bring people together on a specific occasion to collectively acknowledge some milestone.

Both rituals and ceremonies are staged events within an organization, therefore a deliberate cultural activity. Why are they celebrated and what does that mean? Organizations have ceremonies for promotions, retirements, and birthdays. They may be elaborate or more ritualistic. What does the organization choose to celebrate? Are the celebrations focused on individual life milestones, such as birthdays, weddings, childbirth, etc.? Or are the celebrations more organizationally specific such as goal attainment, promotions, and transfers or retirements? Regardless, they are all important sources of information about the company culture and what it chooses to celebrate.

What are the general attitudes and norms displayed by members of the organization? Attitudes are part of others' performances – what are they performing and why? Are they satisfied or dissatisfied with their role in the group or company? Are they *organizational citizens*? If so, what type of citizen are they? Are they exemplars, politicians, slackers, or troublemakers? What are the norms in the organization? Do they differ across role-sets or do they hold constant? Either way, what does that mean? Are there certain unwritten codes for conduct? Are they similar or dissimilar to the written ones? What are the sanctions for violating the norms? What would an external audience think of these norms? Similar to the norms, what are the values held by the organizational members? How are they communicated and how are they rewarded or enforced?

So, how do we become indoctrinated in an organization's culture? *Socialization* is the process by which people, beginning with infancy, learn to become effective participants in social relationships in various contexts. Social psychologists seeking to understand the relationships between individuals, and the different groups to which they belong, have been interested in asking "Who does the socializing?", "What are the processes involved in the socialization?" and "What outcomes are the result of the socialization process?"

Organizational socialization is the process that newcomers in an organization go through on their way to becoming organizational citizens. Organizational socialization can also be a useful perspective when considering organizational culture. In fact, organizational culture may be the single most important learning outcome from the socialization process. So what happens during socialization? Daniel Feldman, a noted scientist in the organizational sciences, suggested that socialization occurs in three primary stages which he named the *anticipatory stage,* the *accommodation stage,* and the *role management stage.*[3]

The *anticipatory socialization stage* refers to all of the knowledge we acquire prior to joining the organization. It includes all that we have been able to gather from others, such as what is generally known about the organization, and even the *reputation* of the organization. An organization's reputation is similar to personal reputation in that it is the sum of all others' impressions of the entity in question – in this case, their impression of the organization. Also, like personal reputation, the organization's reputation has value. All of these form the basis of the degree to which an individual may desire to join the organization. Is the organization highly regarded by others? Is it a desirable company to work for? Is there alignment with what the company does and individual interests? The answers to these and other questions form expectations and help frame decisions about joining the organization.

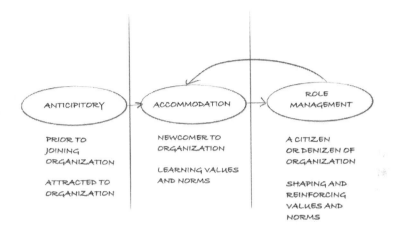

Figure 27: Feldman's Stages of Socialization

Once the decision is made to join an organization, the individual enters into the *accommodation stage*. In this stage, the individual is essentially a newcomer and an information seeker within the organization. This is when the initial role-sets are formed and the networks emerge. Relationships are established, initial social exchanges take place, trust is earned, and reputations start to grow. This is when the newcomer begins to develop skill sets, relationships, networks, spheres of influence, negotiate the various role-sets and resolve role ambiguity, and assesses their own sense of fit and future within the organization. This is also when the early stages of group development (*forming, storming, norming*) emerge.

The final stage of socialization according to Feldman, the *role management stage*, essentially refers to maintaining relationships and mediating conflict between others in the organization. This social stage is marked by the latter stages of group development (*performing* and *adjourning*). This is the realm of politics. How it is played, what it is played for, and who is playing begins to emerge in this stage. Consider our previous discussion on organizational politics. Political activities are defined by the context of the organization. An individual trying to use political influence early in the accommodation stage, would likely not yet have a sufficient grasp of the organization's culture and a sufficient relationship base to be effective. In the role management stage, all of the requisite components for political influence begin to emerge.

So, what does all of this have to do with organizational culture? Socialization answers questions such as "How do we learn organizational culture, when do we learn it, and what is it that we learn?" How socialization is carried out also explains how we behave as citizens of the organization. Are we exemplars? Are we rebels? Do we drink from the "company chalice?" If so, we are likely *organizational citizens*, meaning that we have embraced membership and are now contributors and enforcers of the values and norms of the organization. If we did not drink from the "company chalice," we are likely *denizens* who have taken up temporary residency. It is important to note that while a denizen may perform to appear as a citizen, they have not internalized the norms and values. It is also important to note that a denizen can still become a citizen, and over time likely will.

When applied to organizations, socialization is the process by which individuals are informed of, and subsequently adopt the attitudes, values, and culture of the organization. Organizational socialization is widely recognized as an effective approach to achieving or creating a strong person-organization fit. As new organizational members come to understand the values, abilities, expected behaviors, and social knowledge that are essential for assuming a role in the organization, they move toward value congruence with the organization. In other words, these individuals develop a strong sense of organizational identity. What we have learned is that certain socialization tactics, applied in particular contexts, have predictable outcomes. By institutionalizing such tactics in a system of socialization routines, organizations can achieve high degrees of person-organization fit.

Socialization researchers John Van Maanen and Edgar Schein identified six basic socialization tactics, each one representing a continuum between two extremes of institutional vs. individual socialization.[4] The *collective* versus *individual* tactic refers to the degree to which a group of individuals goes through a common set of experiences together. The *formal* versus *informal* tactic refers to the degree of segregation that occurs between those being indoctrinated and the regular organizational membership. The *sequential* versus *random* tactic represents the degree of formality and the clarity of the boundary passages. The *fixed* versus *variable* tactic describes the temporal aspects of socialization to the degree that there is a specific start and end point, and the points in-between are clearly punctuated. The *serial* versus *disjunctive* tactic reflects the degree to which seasoned members of the organization become active role models for new members. Finally, the *divestiture* versus *investiture* tactic refers to the degree to which the organization is willing to embrace the identity of the individual.

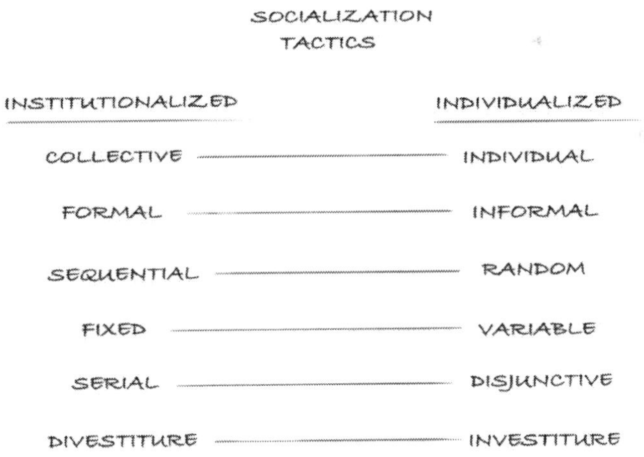

SOCIALIZATION
TACTICS

INSTITUTIONALIZED	INDIVIDUALIZED
COLLECTIVE	INDIVIDUAL
FORMAL	INFORMAL
SEQUENTIAL	RANDOM
FIXED	VARIABLE
SERIAL	DISJUNCTIVE
DIVESTITURE	INVESTITURE

Figure 28: Van Maanen and Schein's Socialization Tactics

Each of these socialization tactics can be represented on a continuum that at one end constitutes an *institutionalized perspective* (one that emphasizes loyalty and fosters a collective identity), and at the other end an *individualized perspective* (one that promotes innovation and individualism). The notion of a continuum is important because it implies that the anchors of the continuum are conceptualized as being mutually exclusive; that is, socialization tactics can be employed to foster an institutionalized perspective or an individualized perspective, but not necessarily both simultaneously.

Ultimately the result of the socialization process, implemented through the tactics described above, is a strong person-organization fit. The notion of "fit" describes the extent that an individual has embraced the organization's culture and values, and behaves in a manner consistent with the expectations of organizational membership. This congruence of the individual and the organization results in trustworthy stewards of the organization's mission, values, and resources, and future exemplars from which subsequent newcomers to the organization can model their own behaviors and expectations.

Edgar Schein suggested that socialization processes operate across the entire range of organizational norms and values, but the rewards for compliance and sanctions for non-compliance differ depending on the importance of the norm, managerial styles, and the organization's culture.[1] He suggested that this variation allows for differences in the outcomes attributed to socialization. A newcomer could embrace none of the values, only the most important ones, or the entire range of values and norms.

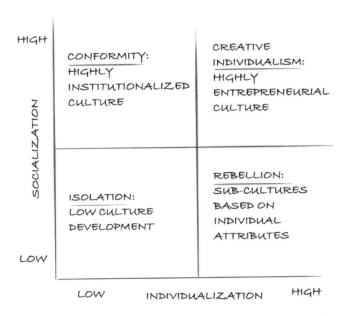

Figure 29: Schein's Socialization and Culture

Schein suggested that the behavioral outcomes associated with these variations resulted in a failure of socialization, in that nonconformity can result in the in the rejection of all values and norms and over-conformity can result in the complete acceptance of all values and norms. He suggested that organizations should be in pursuit of creative individualism, which is the result of embracing the most important values and norms and rejection of the rest. This, he argued, would be an entrepreneurial culture capable of innovation and change.

Adding to the understanding of the outcomes of socialization, researchers have also focused on what is learned by the individual in the process. In other words, what is the content or curriculum of the socialization process? Based on the collective work of many researchers, Georgia Chao and her colleagues suggested there were six categories of learning or content outcomes of organizational socialization: *performance and proficiency, people, politics, language, organizational goals and values,* and *history.*[5] These six categories represent the scope of cultural knowledge gained during socialization.

The *performance and proficiency* category refers to the learning of tasks required on the job as well as the identification of what needs to be learned. This is where we assess the knowledge, skills, and abilities that are needed (or need to be learned) for us to be successful in the organization. We also learn what it will take to be proficient or good at the job. We identify the criteria for performance as it is defined by our role and as valued by the organization. This is where we first start to establish our credibility and expertise.

In the *people* category, the focus is on establishing relationships with other organizational members and finding the right people from which to learn and exchange information about the job and the organization. These relationships can be in the form of work-related or non-work-related relationships. They are the exemplars, the gate-keepers, co-workers, supervisors, people in other departments, etc. Successful learning in this category is a reflection of how well the individual's social skills and behaviors fit within the context of interpersonal, group, and organizational relationships.

The *politics* category includes gaining knowledge about the social landscape and political arena. It includes knowledge of formal and informal work relationships and power structures. Politically socialized individuals learn to navigate the culture and deal with political behavior. Individuals who are well socialized into organizational politics likely have a competitive edge over those who are not. Knowledge of cultural norms and situationally appropriate behavior is essential to success in the political arena. Also, as previously mentioned, the nuanced knowledge of politics category is likely gained in the role-management socialization stage.

The *language* category includes the specific knowledge content of the technical language and jargon of the organization. This is central to organizational socialization, as it is essential to effective communication between organizational members. All organizations develop unique terms and acronyms that, when used in communication between organizational members, serve to identify a degree of knowledge or expertise. Additionally, the language used in an organization can be viewed as a source of common identity among organizational members and, as such, knowledge of organizationally unique language can provide members with a sense of belonging.

The category of *organizational goals and values* includes the tacit goals and values of influential organizational members as well. The information in this category serves as the baseline for an individual to assess how well their individual goals are aligned with the goals and values of the organization. These goals and values go beyond those related to their immediate job or role-sets. This category reflects the contextual information surrounding the individual's role.

The final category, *history,* represents the organization's traditions, customs, myths, and culture. Indeed, imbedded in an organization's history is a plethora of information regarding the organization's culture. As individuals learn of key events and incidents that punctuate the organization's history, they can better understand the context within which their actions and behaviors are interpreted by other members of the organization.

Collectively, these categories of socialization represent the "curriculum" of organizational indoctrination. This "curriculum" includes learning: what tasks are required on the job; the language used in the organization; the organization's traditions, customs, myths, and culture; the organization's goals and values, including the tacit goals and values of influential people; the development of trust with fellow organizational members, and developing a relationship with the best person to learn from. These relationships primarily are the reflection of individual social skill and situationally appropriate behavior. Collectively, the categories of socialization consist of the knowledge required for an individual to successfully become a valued member of the organization.

Organizational culture is an open book ready to be read from a meta-perspective. Take notice of relationships and stories, symbolism, norms, ceremonies, and humor, as all of these are woven into the fabric of the organization's culture – and an understanding of this culture presents a very powerful source of leverage and influence to the sophisticated observer. At the same time, organizational culture can be a significant source of frustration and even social danger to the unwitting.

Culture influences us at the generic and extra-subjective levels of our sensemaking. It contains cues about widely held beliefs, customs, knowledge, and practices. It influences our behavior, even though we seldom examine it explicitly. It provides a sense of stability in an otherwise uncertain environment. It helps us understand others' attitudes and behavior.

A bona fide leader not only has perspective but can view situations from multiple perspectives. Understanding culture, what it is, where it comes from, and how it impacts individual attitudes, opinions, and behavior is critical. They understand that imbedded in the culture are symbols with deep and rich meaning and that invoking that symbolism in communication can have a profound effect. Authentic leaders understand the importance of socializing new members into the organization's culture and that culture becomes a significant source of organizational reputation, which in-turn serves to attract high quality new members.

Dazed and Confused

It was the fourth day on the job and the newbie still felt overwhelmed. She was excited at the prospect of working for this prestigious company and was eager to make a good impression early on. She had met dozens of people so far and could of course only remember of few of their names. They, on the other hand, all knew her because she was the "newbie." She also had a hard time understanding some of the conversations; they used unique terms and acronyms as though it was a common language. She had much to learn.

Regarding the job, she was still a bit unclear on what her role was and what the expectations were, but she felt that would come in short order. She had already made a few friends and they seemed to help her understand what was expected. Whispered comments such as "Don't worry about working on that, this one is the most important." or "Be sure to have your mobile phone ringer turned off, because the Director has a thing about us using our phones at work." all were beginning to fill in the gaps of her knowledge. But she was still the newbie.

In meetings, she wasn't sure where to sit or when to speak. Should she sit at the table, along the wall, in front, or in back? Should she speak out if she had an opinion or just keep her mouth shut. During lunchbreaks, she heard stories about former employees or the past exploits of current employees – some good, some not so good. Should she tell stories about her past experiences or just listen to theirs? She learned about those who had been fired, those who were promoted, who dated whom, and who were the "movers and shakers." She was warned about trusting a particular person too much and advised to avoid working on time-sensitive projects with another.

All of this information was swirling around in the newbie's head. Would she ever be able to comprehend it all? Was this even the right place for her? She sensed that there were pockets of people that were aligned with one another, but it was so nuanced she could not be sure. She felt that for now, the best course of action was to work hard at learning her job, keep a low profile, develop relationships, and the rest would come.

Reflections

Have you been the "newbie"?

What did you learn?

How did you prioritize your learning?

Did you make "newbie" social mistakes?

Who should the newbie seek for mentoring?

What can the newbie do to accelerate her learning?

What can the newbie do to appear credible?

What might undermine the newbie's credibility?

At what point would you suggest the newbie will no longer be a newbie?

References

1. Schein, E.H. and P. Schein, *Organizational culture and leadership*. 5th edition ed. 2017, Hoboken, NJ: Wiley.
2. Cameron, K.S. and R.E. Quinn, *Diagnosing and Changing Organizational Culture: Based on the Competing Values Framework*. 2011: Wiley.
3. Daniel, C.F., *A Contingency Theory of Socialization*. Administrative Science Quarterly, 1976. **21**(3): p. 433.
4. Van Maanen, J. and E.H. Schein, *Toward a Theory of Organizational Socialization*. Research in Organizational Behavior, 1979. **1**: p. 209.
5. Chao, G.T., et al., *Organizational Socialization*. Journal of Applied Psychology, 1994. **79**(5): p. 730-743.

CHAPTER 16

Dramaturgical Perspective

"Through spontaneity we are re-formed into ourselves. It creates an explosion that for the moment frees us from handed-down frames of reference, memory choked with old facts and information and undigested theories and techniques of other people's findings. Spontaneity is the moment of personal freedom when we are faced with reality, and see it, explore it and act accordingly. In this reality the bits and pieces of ourselves function as an organic whole. It is the time of discovery, of experiencing, of creative expression."

—Viola Spolin[1]

We previously discussed the idea of the "presented self." This idea comes from the sociologist Irving Goffman, who suggested that the self can be viewed as the product of the scene that is acted out and not the cause of the scene.[2] This perspective is also useful when considering multiple social interactions within a group of people or between groups of people – in this case the members of an organization. This perspective is typically referred to as a *dramaturgical* perspective.

The notion of a dramaturgical perspective invokes a range of metaphors useful in making sense of organizational occurrences. Performances, scripts, roles, lead actors, supporting actors, sets, props, plots, triumphs and tragedies all come to mind. In the seminal book on the artistry of leadership, *Reframing Organizations: Artistry, Choice, and Leadership*, Lee Bolman and Terrence Deal frame understanding organizations from four different perspectives or frames: *structural, human resource, political, and symbolic.*[3]

From a *structural* frame they argued that leaders focus on influencing behavior through re-designing work relationships and processes; from a *human resource* frame, they suggested that leaders influence change through a focus on meeting employee needs and empowerment of employees; from a *political* frame, leaders influence change through coalition building, selling, and maneuvering; and finally, from a *symbolic* frame, leaders focus on the power of symbolism within the organization to influence change. Similar to Goffman's ideas, when viewing behavior from this last perspective, Bolman and Deal suggest that all social activity within an organization can be viewed as drama.

From a dramaturgical perspective, meaning is derived from the story being performed, the actors delivering the performance, the stage of the performance, and the audience of the performance. From the story perspective, we should ask ourselves "What is the plot? What are the scripts? What are the central roles? Who is the protagonist? Who is the antagonist?" And perhaps more importantly, "Why is the plot like this? Why is the script written as it is and why are certain actors in certain roles?"

When we consider the space, set or "stage" we ask "What does the location have to do with the performance? What are the various props and why are they there? Do they communicate power? Status? Control? Openness? Innovation?" We know from Phillip Zimbardo's prison experiment that the "stage" has a very powerful influence on behavior. It represents something more than the mere "props" would have us believe. Indeed, Zimbardo showed that even when the set was an obvious facsimile of realty, it still invoked profound emotions because of what it represented, what it "said" to the participants and how it informed their role-sets. Guards derived more power and status and prisoners became more dejected. The set and all of its symbolism communicated control.

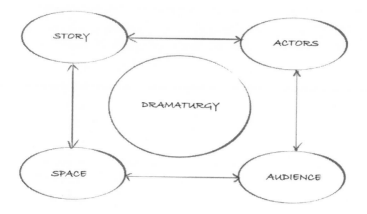

Figure 30: Elements of Dramaturgy

When we think about the audience, what do we know about them? *Why* are they the audience? What do they represent within the organization? Why are they there as an audience? Why aren't they performing? Are they there as social support or do they hope to witness the agony of defeat? Do they believe in the performance? If so, what does that say about them? Do they identify with the actors? If so, what does that say?

Through a dramaturgical lens everything we see is up for interpretation. For every surprise we make a new sense and invent a new understanding. We are at once audience member to others' performances, leading actors in our own performances, supporting actors in others' performances, and even props on the stage. This perspective suggests that much of organizational interaction is ritualistic and symbolic. Everything from the "crisis" presented at the weekly meeting to birthday parties in the break-room are staged performances for effect. It is important to note that this effect may be a good one. This discussion is not implying that there is some sinister force at play duping all of us into compliant organizational citizenship, instead it suggests that for every observed performance there are layers of meaning. In the next chapter we will discuss organizational politics and, central to our discussion on the *political* frame, we will explore how some of us "opt in" and "opt out" of political performances.

Perhaps there is no greater political stage than the seemingly endless array of meetings that punctuate life in organizations. In these meetings, scripts are followed and even impromptu performances are delivered all for the purpose of advancing agendas, either personal or collective, and these agendas are almost always in pursuit, either directly or indirectly, of resources and/or opportunities. Often these meetings result in no actual work being accomplished, rather they present a series of performances, perhaps scenes, that string together to create a production to various audiences. Bolman and Deal even suggested that meetings can be a signal to external audiences that the organization is taking action and is healthy. Consider a scenario in a department that has recently experienced a drop in sales and when asked about it by the CEO, the department manager responds with "We are having a meeting about that issue tomorrow." The effect of knowing a meeting is scheduled looks like action and can actually lead the CEO to *satisfice* that everything is under control. The plot of the performance (the meeting) is to address signal action to the audience (CEO, department members, other stakeholders, etc.). Sometimes just knowing there is a meeting scheduled to address some problem or issue has a placebo effect – we like to think it is working – so, to the degree we believe it, it feels like purposeful action.

Perhaps the most common form of acting in an organization is improvisation, which is essentially how we interact and perform with one another in an impromptu fashion. As defined by Christine Moorman and Anne Miner, improvisation is "the degree to which the composition and execution of an action converge in time."[4] Following this definition, and the assertion that most of our organizational performances are impromptu performances, it suggests that our presented selves are often called upon by our role-sets to serve as supporting cast members in others' performances, and as lead characters in our own, without the benefit of a well-thought-out script. Even when we do have a script to follow, often our supporting actors change the performance we expected them to follow, which thereby forces us to adapt and change our performance.

Improvisation in music, acting, or comedy is viewed as artistic expression. It also has elements of a craft, and like a craft it can be learned through practice over time. Also like a craft, there are certain general rules to guide performances – rules that not only ensure fluidity in individual performances, but also in synchronizing with the performance of another actor. While improvisation sounds freewheeling and completely erratic, it is actually grounded in shared understandings. Each actor choosing to improvise is guided by a sense of their relationship with the other actor or actors; the performance exists for a reason and that reason is a theme around which the performance must orbit. To deviate away from the theme is to deliver a poor performance and render fellow actors vulnerable. In other words, to paraphrase an old saying, improvisation, like creativity, is a *variation of an existing theme.*

Viola Spolin, who has influenced multiple generations of actors, suggested that creativity is not simply a rearrangement of the familiar, rather it is *making the invisible, visible.*[1] Yet another way in which to consider improvisation is to consider it as a conversation. As in any conversation between two people, there is a topic or context, there is a give and take – I say something that begs a response from you, your response then generates a response from me, yet we are conversing around a theme. We can redirect the conversation, and thereby change the theme, but we do so following some mutually understood convention. We use bridges and transitions to signal to the other that we are moving to a different theme.

To practice improvisation, acting coaches and musicians alike suggest following a "yes-and" model.[5] This means when another performer delivers you to an opening in the performance you accept it as it is "yes," then add to it a manner that takes it somewhere new "and." For this to work, our performance cannot be at the expense of other performers – we cannot reject their performance nor hand them back a performance within which they do not fit. To do this will undermine the very nature of the shared performance and it becomes a solo act. Recall reciprocity and reputation here. If you are known as a solo performer, or one that turns a shared performance into a solo performance, you will soon find that most of your performances are solo, as you will no longer be "invited" into others' performances.

Similarly, and for similar reasons, we must not impose our solo performance on the overall shared performance in such a way that dominates the overall performance. Again, think reciprocity, and how our performance must be more than just another line or "treading water." Instead, our performance must build upon the existing performance and create variation around the existing theme. Finally, and much like the avoidance of the "soloist" point, we must not leave co-performers hanging, we must be ready to step in when we sense they are waning in their performance.

All of this give and take, interpretation and variation, is happening in compressed time and while improvisation may seem like non-choreographed spontaneity, it is in reality *rehearsed spontaneity*. Consider the world-class athletes who compete at the highest levels. No basketball, football, or soccer game is completely scripted. All play is improvised around disciplined skill sets and an unwritten yet understood script. The skill sets leveraged in the performance are learned over time and through many repetitious activities or "drills." Consider the basketball player who practices free-throws for hours on end or the soccer player juggling a soccer ball day-after-day. These developed skill sets become the baseline from which the theme and improvisation emerges. Dress rehearsals or scrimmages prepare performers for the real performance, yet as the real performance begins, players improvise within their skill sets and work together to deliver a unique, yet still scripted performance.

Improvisation is something we do many times throughout the day without much thought or consideration of the effect. But if we stop and consider the effect, we can quickly see the value of delivering strong performances. The advantages include increasing our adaptive capacity, enhancement of our collaborative skills, an enriched ability to communicate, an increase in social efficacy, and improved introspection.

Perhaps the most notable benefit is that a good improvisation performance presents us to others as sincere and authentic. For the bona fide leader, this is the essence of leadership. If we are to have "chinks" in our presentation "armor" they will reveal themselves in moments of spontaneity. When these "chinks" appear, they become the triggers that undermine intuitive trust. This suggests that, like the soccer player, bona fide leaders should practice improvisation to better hone their performances.

The Dance

Martin was headed to the meeting. The entire department had been dreading this meeting because rumor had it that the budget had been cut, and that many would exit this meeting without their projects being funded. Martin's good friend Jim was no different. Jim had worked tirelessly on his project proposal and was passionate about seeing it through. He was convinced, as was Martin, that his was one of the most – if not *the* most – important project proposal on the table. The problem was that others had their pet projects as well and there would be winners and losers with not much middle-ground. The spoils would go to the victors, and this was going to be a show-down.

The meeting began in its normal fashion with the director providing an overview of the budget, recent updates, and general information. Then the agenda turned to the project proposals. This is where it would get messy. Jim was expecting strong resistance to his proposal, mainly because it was viewed as one of the front-runners. As his proposal was introduced, he could see the glances and subtle non-verbal signals between would-be adversaries across the meeting room. He braced for the assault.

As if on cue, Martin, who was sitting across the table and three seats to the left of Jim, opened the discussion by questioning Jim about his project's proposed cost. "Are we sure we can afford this?" he asked. "Is it really worth all of the associated costs? Will we see a reasonable ROI?" After a few questions from others in the room, Martin again chimed in. "How is this aligned with our other strategic initiatives? What are the opportunity costs associated with funding this effort? How can we be sure we will even achieve our desired outcomes?" As Martin and several others continued to hurl questions at Jim, others in the room sensed that Martin was actually an antagonist and not necessarily a strong supporter of Jim's project, in fact he almost seemed adversarial.

Following the meeting and the news that Jim's project was among those to be funded, Jim stopped by his friend Martin's office. As he leaned his head in he whispered, "Thanks for the dance old friend, I do not think it would have been approved without your assistance." Martin replied, "Anytime Jim, I believe in the merits of your project and your ability to pull it off."

Reflections

What was the performance?

What was the stage?

Who were the actors?

Who was the audience?

How might this story illustrate improvisation?

Was the performance successful?

Was there likely a rehearsal?

Why was it critical that the performances be authentic?

What were the risks associated with the authentic performance?

How might this story illustrate the principles of "yes-and?"

References

1. Spolin, V., C.B. Sills, and P. Sills, *Improvisation for the theater : a handbook of teaching and directing techniques.* 3rd ed. ed. 1999: Northwestern University Press.
2. Goffman, E., *Theœ presentation of self in everyday life.* Doubleday anchor book. Vol. 174. 1959, New York [u.a.]: Doubleday.
3. Bolman, L.G. and T.E. Deal, *Reframing organizations.* 5. ed. ed. 2013, San Francisco, Calif: Jossey-Bass.
4. Christine, M. and S.M. Anne, *Organizational Improvisation and Organizational Memory.* The Academy of Management Review, 1998. **23**(4): p. 698.
5. Yorton, T. and K. Leonard, *Yes, And: How Improvisation Reverses "No, But" Thinking and Improves Creativity and Collaboration--Lessons from The Second City.* 2015: HarperCollins.

CHAPTER 17

Political Perspective

"Important changes that are shaping the nature of work in today's complex organizations demand that we become more sophisticated with respect to issues of leadership, power, and influence."

—John P. Kotter[1]

"Management is itself a political activity."

—Jeffrey Pfeffer[2]

"Political leaders are advocates and negotiators who value realism and pragmatism. They spend much of their time networking, creating coalitions, building a power base, and negotiating compromises."

—Lee Bolman and Terrence Deal[3]

Organizational politics are not a uniquely contemporary phenomenon. It has been around as long as organizations have. It is fixed feature within organizations. It stems from ideas that have to compete for attention and support. In ancient Greece, Aristotle proposed that politics was a means to create order out of competing interests without the need for totalitarian rule. This suggests that in the interplay of competing interests, organizational politics are a means of influencing decisions. Organizational politics arise from the notion that decisions are often not based on rational thought alone, and when various interests are incongruent political behaviors and persuasion tactics arise to influence those decisions.

An organization is fundamentally a social enterprise. They consist of individuals interacting within a designed structure that is supported by both material and non-material inducements. Organizations are collections of people working towards a common set of goals and objectives. From a political perspective, these social machinations can be viewed as a game. To follow Barnard Suits' definition of "games," he argued that game-playing is a voluntary and deliberate activity designed to overcome unnecessary obstacles.[4] Game-playing and overcoming "unnecessary obstacles," according to Suits, is a central component of human social existence.

As individuals seek to influence outcomes in their work environments, they turn to game-playing and they develop a sense for how to influence those outcomes and they become active in the creation and maintenance of the role-sets that are present in the game's arena. Within these organizational role-sets, individual behaviors that further the goals of the work group or organization are typically referred to as *citizen* behaviors, while individual behaviors in pursuit of individual motives and strategies are commonly referred to as *careerist* or *Machiavellian* behaviors.

The look of organizations, and the game-playing, has changed dramatically from the days of large hierarchically-structured bureaucracies. Contemporary organizations value agility and adaptability. Through extensive down-sizing and restructuring, they are becoming flatter, more matrix-like structures with coordination and control mechanisms operating more horizontally, or omni-directionally, rather than vertically. In these flatter organizational structures, the hierarchical information flow has been replaced with new information pathways or conduits that reflect team-based work structures and redefined role-sets. Employees are expected to perform in fluid and changing roles and possess enough social savvy to understand and manage people in ever-changing organizational settings. It is through the integration of the various role-sets that a rich picture emerges, portraying individuals in organizational settings as both products and purveyors of their environment.

In this new organizational order, social relationships have become an essential currency. Individuals leveraging their influence, both inside and outside of the organization, to accomplish goals and secure scarce resources are the new rainmakers. These social influencers are the organizational stars who always seem to be on the winning team and always seem to get the good projects. They get things done. Interestingly, these "stars" seem to understand the organization's political climate and actually leverage it for the success of the task or project they are pursuing. This implies that organizational politics are the backdrop or arena for social influence behaviors. From a political perspective, social influence behaviors in organizations result from social knowledge gained through sensemaking.

As individuals make sense of their organizations, they are presented with certain opportunities. Employees may actually perceive from their intra-subjective sense, an inter-subjective sense, or even a generic sense, that an organization's reward systems reinforce political behavior. This suggests that knowledge of an organization's political climate is actually *informal curriculum,* implicitly imbedded in an organization's culture and learned in the organization's socialization processes. As such, this learned and reinforced behavior helps to explain why the prevalence of political behavior differs from organization to organization, and even within different levels of the same organization.

This conversation is not intended to portray organizational politics as bad, or something that organizations should seek to eradicate. It is simply that organizational politics exists, in varying degrees, in all organizations. Indeed, an organization without politics is an organization without resources or opportunities. In other words, organizational politics are ubiquitous. Yet, the term "organizational politics" is often misleading. Any attempt to define organizational politics must span all organizational levels to be meaningful as a generalizable concept. It might be simplest to say that organizational politics are a purposeful collection of social influence attempts within an organizational context. It is a refinement of social improvisation skills within the context of the organization.

In hierarchical organizations, individual attitudes toward politics varies at different levels of the organization. In the popular *The Peter Principle* by Laurence Peter and Raymond Hull, they suggested that people in a hierarchy tend to rise to their "level of incompetence".[5] They argued that employees are promoted based on their success in their current role and in their new role they find that the skills from the previous role do not translate and they are no longer competent.

"The Peter Principle" applies to politics as well. Consider a typical hierarchical organization as having three basic levels: *operational, tactical,* and *strategic.* At the *operational* level, focus is typically on production and meeting demands for goods and services. The decisions that are made usually have a horizon of less than 12 months and are often less than one month in scope. The stakeholders at this level largely consist of co-workers, subordinates and supervisors. The work environment is mostly internal, meaning there is not much interaction with external environment and most challenges can be controlled by the organization. Organizational politics as a way to get things done is largely not appreciated at this level, as the emphasis is on production and getting the work done.

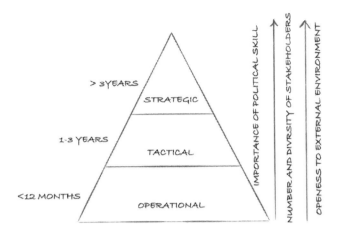

Figure 31: Organizational Politics

The *tactical* level is focused on maintaining and forecasting demand for goods and services. Time horizons at this level go beyond the current year and tend to span out to three years. Stakeholders at this level mostly are industry-related and include customers, suppliers, and vendors, as well as internal organizational stakeholders. Similarly, at this level there is an increasing interaction with the external environment and dealing with issues beyond the direct control of the organization. Organizational politics are viewed as "coming with the job." Having political skill is viewed as a skill set necessary for success as competing interests become more common.

At the *strategic* level of the organization, the focus is on the industry, market conditions, labor conditions, new technologies, and consumer trends. This requires time horizons out beyond three years as decision-makers are challenged with less clarity on the future. Obviously, most of the stakeholders are external to the organization and many even external to the industry and include investors, shareholders, competitors, consumers, politicians, legal advisors, partners, employees, etc. At this level, interactions are mostly with the external environment and are nearly all beyond the direct control of the organization. Political skill is considered an essential skill set at this level and may even be the most important skill.

Revisiting "The Peter Principle," we can see that what makes us successful at one level of the organization does not necessarily prepare us for the rigors of the next. So much so that it is not uncommon in an organization to see newly-promoted personnel struggle to adapt in their new roles. And abundant are the careers that have hit a ceiling due to a lack of political sophistication and a full appreciation of how to perform in the political arena. The good news is that with a sense of purpose, political skill can be developed and practiced in preparation of advancement.

Consider the extensive networks and alliances we form in our different role-sets. These are social investments, relationships, and social exchange with numerous others. Sometimes these others know each other, sometimes they do not. Sometimes they are in competition, sometimes they are in cooperative relationships. Regardless, our political skill enhances our ability to navigate these swirling waters. Our networks and personal reputation both serve to contribute to our accumulation of social capital, and this capital is further enhanced by our political skill. People that possess a high degree of political skill are sophisticated in the management of their multiple social networks. They are careful and selective in the personal investments they make and the relationships they nurture, thereby earning the trust and confidence of others. They are mindful of reciprocity and power relationships. They appreciate the collection of performances that permeate the workplace. Finally, they understand that the single most important component of political skill is relationships. And that those relationships are built on trust.

Gerald Ferris, perhaps the most influential scientist on the topic of politics in organizations, developed the construct of political skill. In his book *Political Skill at Work*, he and his colleagues asserted that political skill is a distinct refinement and deliberate utilization of social skill.[6]

Political skill combines social astuteness with organizational savvy, and an ability to influence others in an apparently sincere (symmetrical) and engaging manner. This earns the confidence and trust of others as behavior is interpreted as genuine. People who possess a high level of political skill know how to emote appropriately in different social situations at work, and they do so in a manner that does not indicate any potentially manipulative motives.

Ferris suggested that there four primary dimensions to political skill: *social astuteness, networking ability, interpersonal intelligence,* and *apparent sincerity*. Politically skilled individuals tend to measure higher on all four dimensions, and varying degrees of ability across the four dimensions result in unique political styles.

Socially astute individuals are those who are very observant of others, and perceive the most subtle cues in social situations. They are sophisticated "readers" of situational dynamics, and are quick to make behavioral adjustments to emote appropriately for the situation. Similar to emotional intelligence, socially astute individuals are typically viewed as being perceptive and clever, and they possess a social sophistication that allows them to navigate complex situations in an appropriate manner. Socially astute individuals are empathetic and particularly good a reading others and calibrating social exchange, as well as understanding the balances across multiple social exchange accounts.

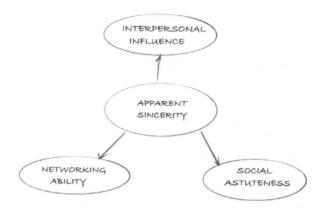

ure 32: Political Skill

The ability to effectively network cannot be overstated. While contemporary social networking sites have radically altered the manner in which people network, it is yet to be understood just how effective vast social networks are. From a political skill perspective, *networking ability* is defined not as a trait, but rather as a type of information power. Politically skilled individuals are very aware of the power of bonding and bridging social capital and they are adept at developing and leveraging this social capital. Effective networkers understand the nature of relationships and what maintenance behaviors need to be exercised to maintain healthy relationships.

Interpersonal influence is the ability to produce a desired attitude change in another person or group of people. As we have previously discussed, individuals who are skilled at influencing others use a blend of ethos, pathos, and logos to win the opinions and attitudes of others. Combined with an engaging personal style, these individuals seem to influence all those around them and are regarded by others as being socially skilled and are particularly adept at nuanced communication. A politically skilled individual asserts influence on others in a manner that is not easily detectable.

Finally, *apparent sincerity* is omnidirectional and must never be compromised. It is an enabler of the other three. Recall the discussion on reputation. To appear sincere, individuals must continuously act in a symmetrically consistent manner, regardless of audience or even the perceived lack of one. Apparent sincerity has a reputational component that if ever violated, will undermine the other dimensions and overall political skill. Individuals possessing a high level of political skill are often perceived as sincere and having a high level of integrity. Due to their social astuteness, they are disarming and invoke trust. They are not perceived as having an agenda or as being manipulative or coercive. Having a high degree of apparent sincerity necessitates an astute understanding of all types of trust, how to gain swift trust, and how to effectively establish identification-based trust and intuitive trust.

As implied by the four dimensions, being politically savvy means ethically generating support for an idea that is important to you. It's about give and take and reciprocity. In fact, linking your agenda with others' agendas in an ethical way is a very powerful approach to building momentum, brainstorming the win-win possibilities, and building action coalitions. Of course, you'll have to establish trust and rapport with your colleagues, be good at managing your impressions, have a good sense of humor, read others' emotions well, and empathize appropriately. You'll need a solid base of social capital, positive reputation, understand organizational culture and power dynamics. You will have to be a convincing performer and present yourself symmetrically and be quick to establish relationships.

So political skill aside, where does one learn the political games? This is one of the primary focuses of mentoring relationships that form during socialization. These relationships produce the organizational knowledge transfer that is necessary for political savvy.[7] Mentors pass along knowledge on office politics and they help manage the protégé's image and visibility within the organization. However, we must recall that a mentoring relationship, like all relationships, is one that is fundamentally based on exchange. To this point, mentors select protégés that they believe can bring certain value in the form of skill, influence, and access to the relationship in order to bring greater rewards to the mentor. From this perspective we can see a mentoring relationship as one based on trust and reciprocity.

The protégés are essentially organizational apprentices who are allowed to "peak behind the curtain" and observe the movements of others in the political arena. It is like a skilled sports announcer pointing out the nuances of a particular play. Mentoring, as a component of the socialization process, is where political skills are developed by protégés. And while those skills are somewhat idiosyncratic to the organization, they are actually quite transferable and may be the most critical set of skills that they acquire in their professional development. In fact, the knowledge gained by protégés is imbedded in organizational context and this context is the necessary backdrop for effective improvisation.

When considering who to choose as a mentor, the protégé seeking political insight is most likely attracted to the mentor's *referent, expert power, informational*, and *connection* power. Referent power is certainly one of the initial attractors to the protégé. But consider how the mentor's expert power helps to provide meaning in ambiguous settings. This is often the primary source of influence wielded by the mentor. From an informational perspective the mentor can be a source of "insider" information that can enhance the protégé's political play. From a connection power perspective, a fundamental aspect of political skill is networking ability, so a mentor's connections are critical to the connectedness of the protégé. Finally, consider the protégé's *reputation* and how it might be shaped simply by having a relationship with the mentor.

As a political player enters into the political arena, their attitude towards politics and the manner in which they engage in politics defines their political style. Joel DeLuca created a taxonomy of political styles base on actors' attitudes toward politics (positive or negative) and the actors' propensity to engage (high or low) in politics.[8] He argued that effective leaders view politics as a positive force and engage in political behavior. He also identified a Machiavellian style where an actor has a negative view of politics but has a high level of engagement.

Regardless of an individual's political skill or political style, politics is an important aspect of social influence in organizations. Indeed, it may be the essence of organizational leadership. Interestingly, the training or teaching of political skill likely is primarily a function of the mentoring process. From a leadership development perspective, what is not obvious is "Who gets the secret handshake?" What are the criteria used to select the fortunate "insiders" and neglect the unfortunate "outsiders"? Perhaps the criterion for "selection" is the quality of social skills and basic ability to influence others. Perhaps then social skill is a pre-requisite of political skill, and political skill is in turn a pre-requisite for leadership.

Bona fide leaders understand the role of politics in organization. They see an arena where good ideas battle for scarce opportunities and resources. Politics are the unwritten rules of the area. Players with integrity compete and champion their ideas. They build coalitions, call in favors (social exchange), and socially maneuver to afford the best opportunity for their idea or agenda to garner support. Bona fide leaders understand that poorly played politics and Machiavellian tactics result in a negative perception of politics but that when played well and with integrity, the best ideas have a chance to rise to the top. Similarly, bona fide leaders are also politically skilled themselves and serve as excellent mentors for schooling future leaders in the realm of politics.

The Golf Tournament

The launch of the new product-line was several months away. The CEO had made it clear to everyone in the organization that this launch was critical to the continued success of the company. All departments were expected to make the launch their number one priority.

The departments, however, did not always communicate well and there were many new personnel who were joining the organization in anticipation of the launch. Obviously the sales department was critical to the launch of the new product-line and they certainly had their share of newbies as well. It was critical that the sales team understood the product and were ready to demonstrate its virtues to their clients.

Eric, Steve, and Frank were the lead salespeople in the department. They also happened to be avid weekend golfers and were always looking for a way to get out during the week. One morning on the way to get a cup of coffee, Eric said "I sure wish we could get out on one of these Fridays for a round of golf." Steve replied "Too bad the boss doesn't play." To that Frank chimed in with "But what if we hosted a golf tournament as a team-building event for the new product launch?" The three continued to discuss the idea and realized that the idea might work, but if they were the planners, they would not be able to play. They needed someone else to run the show and they somehow needed to get on the boss's calendar to pitch the idea.

A few days later, Frank was attending a social event hosted by a private organization that he had joined. The boss happened to be a member as well. He decided to approach the boss in this social setting rather than try to get on her very busy calendar. He waited for the CEO to be free and approached her. He pitched the idea of a team building tournament on a Friday afternoon and she loved it. She told him to get on her calendar sometime in the next week to discuss.

Frank went in the next morning and told Eric and Steve. They were on the hook, but still wanted to play golf. That is when the golfer-guys thought of Dave.

Dave was a quiet, exceedingly competent executive. Dave never boasted or even drew attention to himself, yet everything he was involved in was successful. You could say that Dave's unassuming personality had him flying under the radar. The golfer-guys thought Dave would be perfect to run the tournament and it would serve to bring attention to his competence, something all three believed was important. So they approached Dave about being the lead in planning the golf tournament and Dave was reluctant. He knew nothing about golf. He had never been in a tournament and didn't even play golf.

The golfer-guys promised Dave that they would do most of the work and manage all the details of the tournament from collecting fees to handling catering. All Dave had to do was interface with the boss and on tournament day handle the details while they played golf. After several discussions and a crash course on how it would all work, the golfer-guys and reluctant Dave met with the boss. Dave was introduced as the main planner and organizer and he pitched the idea just as they had rehearsed. The CEO was immediately impressed and agreed to host the event. She asked Dave to get on her schedule again the following week to work out the specifics.

Two months later and after multiple meetings with the boss, it was event day. The guys had delivered on their promise and did all the work. Dave just stood around and greeted folks as they showed up to play. The weather was beautiful, the tournament was full of the company's members, golfers and non-golfers alike, and the catering was on time and delicious. The CEO was ecstatic. When the tournament finished, and as the CEO addressed the company at the luncheon afterwards, she expressed her excitement about the launch of the new product-line and how the golf event was a perfect opportunity for the organization to kick off the launch. She went on to sing the praises of Dave, who had masterfully planned and executed the wonderful event. It was in her words "one of the best events" she had been a part of in a long time and it was "due to Dave's high level of competence and attention to detail."

Several months later, the CEO was looking to fill a newly created position necessitated by the success of the new product-line. This critical and highly visible position demanded an individual that possessed a high degree of professionalism and competence. She could think of no one better than Dave. Three years later, Dave was appointed Vice President of Sales.

Reflections

Was this an example of organizational politics?

Was it a performance?

Who were the political players?

What was the political agenda?

Was the performance deceptive?

If so, was it unethical?

How might this story relate to:

Social Exchange? Dramaturgy? Relationships? Trust? Reputation? Power?

References

1. Kotter, J.P., *Power and influence*. 1985: Free Press.
2. Pfeffer, J., *Managing with power : politics and influence in organizations*. 1992: Harvard Business School Press.
3. Bolman, L.G. and T.E. Deal, *Leadership and Management Effectiveness: A Multi-Frame, Multi-Sector Analysis*. Human Resource Management, 1991. **30**(4): p. 509-534.
4. Suits, B.H., *The grasshopper : games, life, and Utopia*. 1978: University of Toronto Press.
5. Peter, L.J. and R. Hull, *Theœ Peter principle*. 9. print. ed. 1970, New York: Bantam Books.
6. Ferris, G.R., S.L. Davidson, and P.L. Perrewt, *Political Skill at Work*. 2010, Mountain View, CA, USA: Davies-Black Publishing.
7. Ferris, G.R., *Political skill in organizations*. Development and Learning in Organizations: An International Journal, 2008. **22**(1).
8. DeLuca, J.R., *Political Savvy*. 1999, Berwyn, Pennsylvania: Evergreen Business Group.

CHAPTER 18

Followership Perspective

"Followers act as a check and balance on a leader's power, protecting the organization against abuse of the power."

—Peter Northouse[1]

The recognition of *followership* as an important area of study has only recently emerged. To date, almost all attention has been devoted to studying *leadership*. Yet a challenge in studying leadership is that it is largely defined by context and context is undergoing near constant change. Workforces are more diverse. They are multicultural and heterogeneous, they are increasingly informed and more socially complex, they are more collaborative and team-oriented. Reciprocity, trust and relationship building are at an all-time premium.

Vibrant interpersonal relationships between leaders and followers are increasingly being recognized as the pathway to high performing work teams. Yet those interested in studying leadership have historically focused on the leader as the unit of analysis. From this perspective the leader is the individual that creates the vision, defines the mission, and motivates others to action. While this is useful, who is motivated? What are they motivated to do? And why are they motivated? All these questions seem to be unanswered by this perspective. Perhaps a useful alternative perspective is to take a look at the who, what, and why of followership.

In an effort to better understand high performing teams, Robert Ginnett, a leading researcher on leadership, studied pilots and airline crews to determine the behavior of the most effective crew leaders.[2] He found that the most effective crew leaders were those who treated subordinate crew members as partners. He noted that these "partners" were more engaged in informing the leader on critical elements of the operation. More importantly he noted that it was the leader who had created this environment of a partnership. In other words, effective leaders create environments that lead to effective followership.

So then, what is effective followership? How might effective followership be developed and fostered? Are some leaders more effective than others at developing effective followers? If so, what makes them so? Certainly, organizations can be successful with the traditional hierarchical approach to leadership-followership. And while this somewhat simplistic view has historically been the dominant view, it does overlook the critical role of the followers' collective action. In the ever-changing contexts that define the success and failure of leadership, Ginnett's "leader-follower partnerships" provide a much richer vantage point to understanding contemporary leadership. So, before we jump into the *leadership perspective*, we will take a pause and try to understand the *followership perspective* first.

According to Robert Kelley, author of *The Power of Followership*, effective followers are those individuals who are perceived as engaging in "enthusiastic, intelligent, and self-reliant participation—*without star billing*—in the pursuit of an organizational goal."[3] Kelley identified a useful 2x2 for distinguishing follower types. The first dimension is a measure of the individual's level of *independence* and *critical thinking*. The other dimension is a measure of the individual's propensity to be an *active* or *passive* follower. Based on the degree to which followers possess these two attributes, Kelley suggested that a leader will need to call upon different leader behaviors to be effective.[4]

The five different follower types according to Kelley are *sheep, yes-people, pragmatics, alienated followers,* and *effective followers*. Obviously he suggests that the best followers are those who are active critical thinkers. Reviewing each follower type reveals a wide range of leadership skills necessary for leaders to be effective.

The *sheep*, are defined as having low critical thinking, and being passive followers. These individuals require leaders to motivate them and require oversight and supervision.

The *yes-people* are lower in critical thinking yet active followers. They are conformists who are committed to the leader and agree with the goals or tasks being pursued. These followers will defend the leader even when others criticize them, and they typically do not question the leader's decisions or actions.

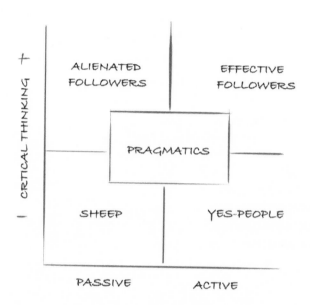

Figure 33: Thinking-Action Followership Grid

The *pragmatics,* which are in the middle with moderate levels of each dimension, are not typically out in front with new ideas nor do they like significant deviations from the norm until others have expressed support. They often prefer to stay in the shadows and, as their plot on the 2x2 grid would suggest, in the middle of the pack.

The *alienated*, which score high on independence and critical thinking, yet passive on the passive/active scale, tend to be negative naysayers and often attempt to subvert the leader by constantly questioning leader decisions and actions. These critical spectators are quick to complain, yet slow to take initiative.

Finally, the *effective followers*, those who are active critical thinkers and active, are the exemplars. They have a positive outlook, are action-oriented, and think critically. They will not categorically accept the decisions or actions of a leader. Instead, they will critically evaluate them and then earnestly pursue them.

Effective followers are stable and responsible actors who pursue goals and objectives without a high need for leader interaction. These are the folks that successful leaders often give credit to for the success of the organizations. Sayings like "get the right people on the bus," or "build a championship team," are references to finding and empowering effective followers. In organizations with a high number of effective followers, a leader tends to be more of a guide and visionary than a hands-on, in-the-trenches manager. As organizational structures flatten, the importance of finding and developing effective followers will become increasingly important. Perhaps most important is the ability to mentor and select future leaders from the ranks of the effective followers.

Whether we find ourselves in a leader or follower role, how we make sense intra-subjectively and with others will define our situation. Because of this, we must be critical thinkers to be effective followers, and effective followers to be effective leaders. Leadership is not some simple list of rules or laws to be obeyed, or even a single theory that wraps up the construct in some neat and tidy package, rather it is a long and often messy journey of self-reflection, learning, and critical thinking.

Earl Potter and his associates describe a somewhat similar approach to followership studies but rather than "critical thinking" and "participation" as the dimensions, they looked at r*elationship initiative* and *performance initiative*.[5] From Potter's perspective, effective followership is about individual performance and taking ownership of the relationship they have with their leaders.

Followers with high *performance initiative* would be characterized as being committed to the highest levels of effort, including working effectively with others, embracing change, doing the job well, and being a valuable contributor. Followers with high performance initiative tend to be team builders who are future-oriented and always striving to do better.

Those followers with a high *relationship initiative* take the responsibility to establish and nurture effective working relationships with their leaders. They pursue openness and understanding within those relationships and seek to inform their own organizational perspectives. A high relationship initiative is marked by trust-building, honest communication, leadership buy-in, and adopting the leader's perspective and priorities.

Potter and his associates labeled the resulting quadrants as *subordinates, contributors, politicians,* and *partners.* With each of these follower types they characterized specific attributes. The *subordinates,* who are traditional followers, tend to be content to do whatever they are told. The *contributors* are focused on performance and are often the workhorses and innovators in an organization. The *politicians* are more concerned with relationships than they are with actual performance. And finally, the *partners* blend superior performance and healthy relationships to positively influence both leaders and peers. We'll take a look at each in greater detail.

The *subordinate* is a follower who does what they are instructed to do. They perform at a competent and satisfactory level but are not well-equipped to deal with change or novel situations. They need checklists. These folks perform well enough to keep their jobs and may even get promoted in a seniority-driven organization, but they typically do not invest in relationship building nor do they pursue high performance.

The *contributor* is a follower who delivers exemplary work. Yet this follower rarely tries to see things from the perspective of the leader. They generally wait for the leader to direct them to new challenges. Although this person is a hard and effective worker, their lack of leadership empathy and relationship building, tend to make them more immediate in their focus and limits the sharing of their expertise and knowledge. Contributors pose a leadership challenge to develop them into fully engaged organizational citizens.

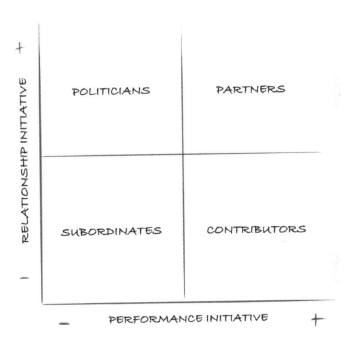

Figure 34: Potter's Followership Grid

Conversely, the *politician* (not to be confused with political skill) gives more attention to managing relationships than to maximizing performance. This person possesses valuable interpersonal qualities that make them well-liked and sensitive to interpersonal dynamics. They can be effective followers in that they provide valuable assistance to the leader in the form of insights and group dynamics. Yet these followers neglect the performance aspects of their jobs in favor of the more social. Since politicians often have well-developed networks, they can be valuable during times of organizational change and crisis management.

Finally, *partners* are those who have a strong desire to do the job that they are assigned and are also attentive to the purpose of the organization. Partners understand, buy into, and communicate the goals of the leader and use this understanding to focus their own efforts. Partners look to become the high performers and master the skills required for their job while also actively pursuing relationship development with the boss to better understand their boss's agenda and the strategy for accomplishing that agenda.

What these two prominent approaches (Kelley's and Potter's) illuminate is that effective followers are those with a high commitment to the mission or purpose of the organization, and they are adaptable and team-oriented. They are also independent critical thinkers and sophisticated social actors with a highly developed sense of integrity and competency. Essentially, effective followers are future leaders awaiting the call to leadership.

Bona fide leaders come from the ranks of effective followers – likewise, effective followers are bona fide leaders awaiting the call. Authentic leaders understand that their leadership is buoyed by followership. Without followers, leaders simply do not exist. Both Kelley's and Potter's ideas on effective followership reveal that an effective follower is a critically thinking, socially astute, action-oriented high performer. This type of followership should be afforded a certain degree of credibility, provided with some measure of autonomy, and provided with ample information and resources to perform to their fullest. Bona fide leaders do this as a way of being. Bona fide leaders need effective followers who in turn need bona fide leaders.

The Mall

(Inspired by Jerry B. Harvey's Abilene Paradox)[6]

The rain was steady, but not heavy. The forecast called for the temperature to top out in the low 70s and for the rain to continue until evening. The four students sharing a beach condo during spring break were certainly not going to walk on the beach today. Though no one discussed it, each of them felt it was a welcome respite from too much sun and too much fun.

Temporarily alone in their thoughts, each of the four were thinking of ways to mope through the day, and each of them was secretly looking forward to some lazy time when the marketing major said "Does anyone want to go to the mall?" She really did not want to go herself, but she was just trying to think of something they could all do together. The political science major, trying to be accommodating said, "That's always an option and we haven't been there yet." The communications major, despite looking forward to reading her novel, but not wanting to go against the group said, "Sure, I'm OK with that, if that's what everyone wants to do." Lastly, the history major who had really wanted to watch a movie chimed in with, "I kind of wanted to visit that mall at some point while we're here anyway."

The traffic was heavy and slow with all of the spring-breakers and vacationers out and about looking for something to do. The mall parking lot was crowded and the rain continued steadily. The typical mall food places all had lines longer than their mediocre food warranted, and the mall stores were all the usual suspects and nothing they did not have back home. They all arrived back at the condo late in the afternoon, having wandered about and not purchasing much of anything.

The history major, trying to make small talk, said, "Well we can check that box." The communications major replied and said "Actually, I would rather have stayed at the condo and read my book, but I went along since everyone was so enthusiastic." Then the political science major chimed in and said "I wasn't too excited about going to the mall, they're all the same to me. I only went because you all wanted to." The marketing major then said "I only suggested it because I thought everyone was going to be bored staying at the condo."

The four students sat back, perplexed that collectively they decided to go to the mall when none of them really wanted to. They each would have preferred to sit around the condo, but for some strange reason they each had chosen to accommodate their misperceived desire of the group.

Reflections

Is this an example of groupthink?

How can all members of a group follow a course of action that none desired?

What were the students following?

How would a leader have made a difference?

How might consensus be different than purpose?

Have you ever contributed to consensus in spite of your own desire?

How could this scenario have turned out differently?

References

1. *Leadership: Theory and Practice, 8th Edition.* 2018, Ringgold, Inc.

2. Ginnett, R.C., *First Encounters of the Close Kind: The Formation Process of Airline Flight Crews.* 1987, Yale University. p. 1-260.

3. Kelley, R.E., *Theœ power of followership.* 1st ed. ed. 1992, New York: Doubleday/Currency.

4. Kelley, R.E., *In Praise of Followers.* Harvard Business Review, 1988. **66**(6): p. 142-148.

5. Potter, E.H., W.E. Rosenbach, and T.S. Pittman, *Followers for the times.* 5th Ed. ed, ed. W.E. Rosenbach and R.L. Taylor. 2001, Boulder, CO: Westview Press. 142-148.

6. Harvey, J.B., *The Abilene Paradox: The Management of Agreement.* Organizational dynamics, 1988. **17**(1): p. 17-43.

CHAPTER 19

Ethical Perspective

"Life is about choices and choices have consequences."

—James Parco[1]

As we have already discussed, trust is a critically important concept in organizations and in life. Trust is our measure that another will act according to some set of shared personal values, morals, or ethics. Yet what are values, morals, and ethics? How are they different? Where do they come from? And how do they guide our behavior? To better understand these "guides" it is useful to understand the difference between them and to appreciate their impact on our behavior and the behavior of others.

First, and perhaps the most diverse, personal values are the beliefs held by individuals or groups that represent some emotional investment, typically made over time and used in distinguishing between what we "should do" and "shouldn't do." Our personal values represent our life experiences and the social forces that influence us. They are a part of our "intra-subjective sense" and are used by us to make new sense and guide our actions on a daily basis. They are the rules by which we make decisions about right and wrong, good and bad. They are our beliefs about what is important and they define our actions. They tend to be hierarchically arranged so that they can help us prioritize which value is more important when we are faced with value conflict. If we violate our values, we face cognitive dissonance and have to either redefine our values or rationalize why the violation was just. Similarly, when we are faced with social situations that push us to violate our values, we face person-role conflict.

While personal values represent our intra-subjective sense, morals are more socially constructed. They tend to be more universal and have broad acceptance. While values are about beliefs, and I can believe differently from you and we can still be in a positive personal relationship, morals are more about objective good and bad, right and wrong. Our morals are the foundation of our reasoning and are influenced by our inter-subjective, generic-subjective, and extra-subjective sensemaking. This means we place more emphasis on our perception of others with regards to their morals. Our fundamental assessment of another individual's trustworthiness is based on a shared set of morals. Morals influence our actions because they provide staunch boundaries for behavior. If two people vary widely on the morals they adhere to, a positive personal relationship may not even be possible.

While values and morals are often implicit and privately held, ethics are an explicitly negotiated sense of right and wrong held by members of a role-set, an organization, or a profession. From this perspective, ethics can be viewed as primarily generic-subjective sensemaking. However, it should be noted that all three (values, morals, and ethics) co-exist and co-influence behavior. Ethics, which are based on moral reasoning, tend to be negotiated and codified into a formal system or set of rules. Consider medical ethics or legal ethics. To violate an ethical code is to violate terms of a profession or to be considered unprofessional. Ethical codes serve to help us do the right thing, especially when faced with a person-role conflict.

But "doing the right thing" can sometimes be a difficult determination when we are in the mode of competing vigorously. When faced with an unclear way forward, we turn to one of two primary perspectives that can result in different interpretations or "guides" for our behavior. The first is based on the idea of *deontological* ethics, which are commonly associated with the writings of Immanuel Kant. A deontological approach asserts that some actions are wrong regardless of the outcomes resulting from that behavior. From this perspective, intent is of the utmost importance, and the consequences of our decisions and behavior do not solely determine whether it is good or bad. In other words, the motive for behavior is the primary determinant of good and bad or *the means justify the ends.*

However, the other perspective is based on consequentialism or *teleological* theories of ethics. According to these theories, actions are judged based on outcomes. Sometimes referred to as a utilitarian perspective, because the behavior is judged based on the creation of the most good or utility or *the ends justify the means*. To illustrate the difference between these two perspectives, consider the act of deception. A deontologist would argue that it is always wrong because the intent is to deceive and misrepresent truth through commission or omission. Yet a teleological approach would argue that deception is wrong only when it results in bad outcomes, such as hurting another, and in certain situations it might even be right based on the good it produces.

If our morals – and hence our moral reasoning ability – are the foundation of our values and ethics, how do we come to possess them? Lawrence Kohlberg suggested that moral reasoning has six distinct stages of development, grouped into three general levels, and that each stage of development is more sophisticated at reasoning moral dilemmas than the one before it.[2] Kohlberg argued that we develop through the six stages progressively; this means that no stage can be skipped. He also argued that once a moral perspective is gained, it is highly unlikely to regress.

Kohlberg's six stages are grouped into three general levels: *preconventional, conventional* and *post-conventional*. The pre-conventional level is largely representative of our childhood and marked by egocentrism. At this level, moral reasoning is a function of direct consequences.

Stage one is *obedience*. In this stage, moral reasoning is a calculus based on punishment or admonishment. Bad behavior is judged based on the severity of the punishment, with more severe punishment being indicative of worse behavior.

In stage two, or *self-interest*, the calculus is based on reward or measurement of positive outcome. Good behavior is measured by degree of good outcome. While stage one reasoning is almost exclusively egocentric, stage two begins to acknowledge social exchange and that through others, one can achieve good outcomes.

As children mature into adolescents, they typically move from pre-conventional to the conventional level of moral reasoning. At this level there is an increased recognition of society's views and expectations. At this level moral reasoning is marked by an adherence to rules and norms even without the presence of explicit rewards for obedience or consequences for disobedience.

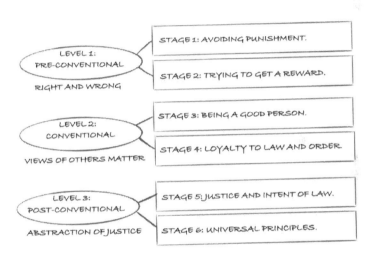

Figure 35: Kohlberg's Stages of Moral Reasoning

Stage three, or *conformity*, is marked by recognition of social roles, role-sets, and expectations. This level of moral reasoning is influenced by an individual's desire for social approval or avoidance of social disapproval. In other words, this stage is largely governed by relationships.

The defining feature in stage four, *law-and-order*, is that moral reasoning acknowledges the importance of obeying laws and social conventions because of their centrality to maintaining society. There is recognition that certain societal needs transcend individual needs, and an acknowledgement that social order is only maintained when members of society follow laws and rules. According to Kohlberg, this is as high a level of moral reasoning that most people ever achieve.

Kohlberg argued that the highest level of reasoning is largely governed by the realization that individuals are distinct from society and that distinction may take precedence over a societal one. From this *post-conventional* level, moral reasoning may guide an individual to disobey rules or norms inconsistent with their own principles. Individuals that reason at this level recognize the utility of rules and norms in maintaining social order, but do not view them as absolutes. Kohlberg suggested that many people will never arrive at this level of moral reasoning.

In stage five, *human rights* level, the perspective is one of a world which consists of a multitude of complex social milieus, each holding different norms, opinions, rights, and values. Laws are regarded as mechanisms or tools to govern human behavior to the benefit of society, and those laws that are not beneficial should be changed to create the greatest good. This level of reasoning follows a teleological line and is arguably the reasoning used to justify democratic governance.

Finally, in stage six, at the *universal human ethics* level, moral reasoning is abstract and invokes principles such as justice. This level of moral reasoning is guided by a deontological perspective. Individual behavior is a function of what is morally right and not a function of instrumentality, normality, or legality. Although Kohlberg argued that this existed, it has been found difficult to demonstrate that it is a static state of moral reasoning.

Our values, morals, and ethics – and the values, morals, and ethics of others – are important to understand in order to effectively influence. We must understand what our guides for behavior are, as well as the guides for others. Consider the impact of values, morals, and ethics on sensemaking. Consider their fundamental influence on trust calculations. Reputations are largely based on behavior that is either consistent or inconsistent with values, morals, and ethics. Relationships are held together, persuasion is enhanced, power is wielded, politics are judged, and leadership is granted based on assessments of values, morals, and ethics.

Effective leaders understand the importance of morals, values, and ethics in their own conduct. They make value-congruent decisions and have a sense for where the boundaries are. Indeed, one of the four main tenets of authentic leadership is having an "internal moral perspective." Also known as *moral reasoning*, bona fide leaders understand that many decisions transcend simple black and white framing, and as such developing a high level of moral reasoning enables selfless decision-making that promotes justice and serves the greater good of their followers. Bona fide leaders understand that what's important is how an issue is framed and what criteria are evaluated for measuring a "good decision."

Dilbert's Dilemma

Dilbert's Dilemma is based on "The Heinz Dilemma," a common exercise used to illustrate Lawrence Kohlberg's stages of moral development.[3]

Dilbert was a working-class man and he and his wife lived on a modest income. His wife, however, was near death and her only hope was a very expensive elixir made from an exotic and very rare blend of cacti. The recipe for this elixir was a closely guarded secret and only recently discovered by an anthropologist studying early Native American culture. Essentially, the elixir costs $10,000 to make, and the anthropologist was selling it for 10 times that at $100,000. Cleaning out all of his savings and retirement accounts, Dilbert could only raise half of the money and his insurance wouldn't make up the difference. He offered $50,000 to the anthropologist, which was still a 500% mark-up, but his offer was rejected. Dilbert even offered to set up a payment plan to cover the difference, but still the anthropologist refused. In desperation, Dilbert considered stealing the drug.

Reflections

Would it be wrong for Dilbert to steal the drug? Why? Why not?

How would this be framed from each of the levels of moral reasoning?

Is the anthropologist justified in her pricing?

Had you assumed the anthropologist was a male? Why? Why not?

Are there hierarchies in moral action?

Which of the following justifications most closely matches yours:

As you consider this moral dilemma, it is important to note that when using Kohlberg's theory, you are interested in what reasoning you used, not the decision that you made.

Stage one (avoiding punishment): Dilbert should not steal the medicine because he could be punished. Or, Dilbert should steal the medicine because if he did not, his wife would die and that would cause him a lot of pain.

Stage two (trying to get a reward): Dilbert should steal the medicine because he will be rewarded with his wife's continued health. Or, Dilbert should not steal the medicine because he would be able to stay free (not in prison), and he cherishes his freedom.

Stage three (being a good person): Dilbert should steal the medicine because as her husband it is his responsibility to take care of his family and be a good husband. Or, Dilbert should not steal the drug because stealing is wrong and he does not want to be that kind of person.

Stage four (loyalty to law-and-order): Dilbert should not steal the medicine because it would be breaking the law. Or, Dilbert should steal the drug for his wife, but also pay for breaking the law.

Stage five (justice and intent of law): Dilbert should steal the medicine, because a right to life is a fundamental human right, and law cannot deny that right. Or, Dilbert should not steal the medicine because the scientist has property rights and is due fair compensation.

Stage six (universal principle): Dilbert should steal the medicine, because preserving a human life trumps the property rights of another person. Or, Dilbert should not steal the medicine, because others may need the medicine just as badly, and their lives are equally significant.

References

1. Levy, D., J. Parco, and F. Blass, *The 52nd Floor: Thinking Deeply About Leadership*. 2008.
2. Kohlberg, L. and R.H. Hersh, *Moral Development: A Review of the Theory*. Theory Into Practice, 1977. **16**(2): p. 53.
3. Kohlberg, L., *The Philosophy of Moral Development*. Vol 1 ed. Essays on Moral Development. 1981, SanFransisco, CA: Harper-Row. 441.

CHAPTER 20

Leadership Perspective

"The key to successful leadership today is influence, not authority."

—Ken Blanchard[1]

"All of the great leaders have had one characteristic in common: it was the willingness to confront unequivocally the major anxiety of their people in their time. This, and not much else, is the essence of leadership."

—John Kenneth Galbraith[2]

"The essence of leadership is not giving things or even providing visions. It is offering oneself and one's spirit."

—Lee Bolman & Terence Deal[3]

We have finally arrived at the leadership discussion, but what is leadership? Can we define it as a construct? Merriam-Webster's dictionary says the word "leadership" is a noun and that it is defined as: "1) the office or position of a leader, 2): capacity to lead, or 3) the act or an instance of leading."[4] It also notes that the first known use of the word leadership was in 1765 in the context of the first definition above. Does that mean it did not exist prior to 1765? Of course not, but what word did we use to convey the office, capacity, or instance of leading?

Since in the definition itself, the words leading, leader, and lead were used, let's see if an understanding of those words can shed light on the word leadership. According to Merriam-Webster, leader, a noun, is defined as a person who leads as: "1) a guide or conductor, 2) a person who directs a military force or unit, or 3) a person who has commanding authority or influence." Leading, an adjective, is defined as: "1) coming or ranking first, 2) exercising leadership, 3) providing direction or guidance, or 4) given most prominent display." Finally, "to lead," a verb, is defined as "1) to guide on a way especially by going in advance 2) to direct on a course or in a direction or 3) to serve as a channel for moving in a certain direction."[4]

So, what is leadership? In Merriam-Webster's attempt to define the word, it used a noun, an adjective and a verb in its various definitions. It is interesting that this word is so difficult to define with any precision, yet many experts profess to know what it is and just how to do it. Thousands of books have been written on the subject of leadership and numerous theories have been presented, all trying to explain what leadership is. Perhaps a quick review of those theories will provide us with the insight to better understand the construct of leadership.

The "great man theory" was based on studying existing leaders who at the time were mostly from the privileged class. This contributed to the notion that genetics or heredity may be involved (i.e. great leaders are born, not made). The great man theory is a nineteenth-century idea, popularized by the writings of Thomas Carlyle in the mid-1800s, which looked at history and historical figures to explain the impact of great men, or "heroes."[5] The theory proposed that highly influential individuals who, due to certain personal characteristics such as charisma, intelligence, wisdom, or social skill, leveraged what we now call social power in a way that had a decisive historical impact. From this perspective, leaders were born and not made, and through their personal prowess they shaped the world around them.

Following this same line of reasoning, Francis Galton suggested that "trait theory" explained leadership. He suggested that people are born with certain "immutable" traits and among those traits are some that make for better leaders.[6] The idea was that if we could just identify the specific leadership traits, then we could find those people with those traits and we would have our leaders – again, leaders are born, not made.

One of the first to criticize trait theory was philosopher and sociologist Herbert Spencer, who suggested that such a perspective was far too simplistic and that sociological forces such as learning, life experiences, and the environment led to the development of people with certain leadership skills.[7] In other words, men were not born with their greatness, rather, the world shaped them so. Spencer argued that such great men are the product of their societies, and that their actions would be impossible without the social conditions built before their lifetimes. Although this perspective would give rise to the "behavioral theories" of leadership, trait theory remained a popular viewpoint until well into the mid 1900s.

The behavioral theories departed from the trait approach and suggested that leaders were in fact made by the life experiences that shape behavior. They suggested that leadership is a definable, learnable behavior. This also differs from the traits theories which looked at who leaders are, by instead looking at what leaders do. Among the behavior theories is the "role theory" of leadership. The role theory of leadership, similar to our discussions on role expectations, suggests that people define roles for themselves and others based on social learning (remember social learning theory) and reading situations. From this perspective, leaders and leader behavior comes from understanding and fulfilling the expectations of others.

Yet others have tried to catalogue the range of leader behaviors or styles and have coined such terms as *autocratic leadership*, which is when a leader makes decisions autonomously and without consulting with others. A *democratic* style is when the leader involves other people in the decision-making. A *laissez-faire* style is described as minimal involvement by the leader in decision-making, thereby allowing people to make their own decisions.

Theorists of "situational leadership" took the idea of different leadership styles and suggested that certain situations called for certain styles of leadership to be effective. They suggested that effective leaders understand that there are multiple factors which affect decisions and these factors, among other things, include the motivation and capability of followers. This implies that the attributions the leader makes regarding the followers will affect what they do and how they lead. Additionally, the leader's perception of themselves, and other factors such as how they make sense and how they interpret the situation, will influence their behavior. A popular approach to emerge from the situational theories is "path-goal theory." Path-goal theory suggests that effective leadership involves encouraging and supporting followers in achieving their goals by making the path toward that achievement clear and unobstructed.

The "contingency leadership" theorists[8] suggested that a leader's ability to lead is based on an amalgam of factors, including the leader's preferred style, the perceived capabilities and behaviors of followers, and situational factors such as the task to be completed or the nature of the task environment. Contingency theories are technically a class of behavioral theory in that the assumption is that there is no one best way of leading, and that a leadership style which is effective in some situations may not be successful in others.

As leadership theories became more complex (i.e. from the simplistic great man theory to the complex contingency theories), the trend in leadership thinking was moving towards an ever-increasing realization that leadership was, at its core, an exchange between leader and follower – recall the ideas discussed in trust and social exchange. Leader-member exchange theory (LMX) suggests that leaders in groups maintain their position of leadership through a series of tacit dyadic exchange agreements with their members.

LMX theory suggests that leaders often have relationships with an inner circle of trusted lieutenants, assistants and advisors, to whom they give high levels of responsibility, decision influence, and access to resources (note the words "relationships" and "trust" in the definition of leader-member exchange). In exchange for this social power (think of all the types of social power), these trusted inner-circle members give back in exchange their trust, loyalty, and followership. Although the leader assumes the dominant role in forming the dyad, and selects members based on a myriad of qualities ranging from personal liking to conscientiousness and competence, followers also choose to enter the relationship based on trust, leader reputation, and perceived competence of leader.

Recall the discussion on relationships. If we are to consider the follower-leader dyad a relationship, then the five necessary conditions for a relationship must be met. First, the dyadic requirement is met by the distinction of the leader-follower dynamic. Next is the mutual acknowledgement, which implies that both the follower and leader acknowledge their respective roles and are in agreement about them. Third, there is a beginning, a sense of time, and perhaps a mutually visualized end state. Fourth, both have expectations of the relationship and those expectations are known. Finally, the relationship exists within a context and is largely defined by that context.

Also consistent with the discussion on organizational socialization and the *accommodation* and *role management* stages, these relationships typically start very soon after a person joins the group and they are marked by three stages of development:

- *Role taking*, where role-sets are first joined. This is where the follower acknowledges their role as follower and recognizes the leader is in the leader role. It is assumed that both leader and follower recognize this dynamic and require the other to perform in their respective roles.
- It is during this *role making*, when role-sets are negotiated, that trust is established and the nature of exchange is tacitly negotiated.
- Finally, *routinization* occurs when the leader-follower relationship, trust and exchange all become established, and the leader-follower exchange defines the effectiveness and capability of the leader-follower role-set.

A popular contemporary theory on leadership is "transformational leadership." Typically contrasted against transactional leadership, in which leader behaviors are viewed as a series of transactions such as punishments and rewards (think transactional trust, reward and coercive power), transformational leadership assumes that followers will follow a leader who inspires them, has a vision and passion, and is someone they believe can achieve great things. Transformational leadership starts with the development of a vision, a view of the future that will excite and convert potential followers. An important point here is that the leader must have social and political skill, high EQ, have perfect symmetry in his or her performance, and illicit trust. Any indications that the leader does not believe in the vision, or is in any way inauthentic, and the followers will be lost.

Once the leader establishes and believes in the vision, they must sell it to their followers. This is an ongoing effort that takes sustained energy and commitment by the leader. For the transformational leader to be effective, trust must be created and maintained through relationships with followers. The transformational leader seeks to continuously inspire followers with a high level of commitment to the vision. Consider here the power of culture that can be brought to bear for this purpose. Transformational leaders understand the needs of their followers, appreciate the power of symbolism in their communications, and understand the dramaturgical aspects of their own performances and that of the organization. They leverage the meaning inherent in ceremonies, rituals and other cultural symbolism to sustain momentum. They are social alchemists who resist simple characterizations.

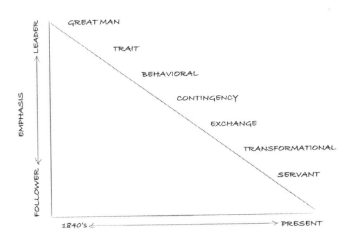

Figure 36: Leadership Theories

Servant leadership is perhaps the most recent theory of leadership which suggests the most effective leaders are those who focus on serving their followers. According to this most follower-centric theory of leadership, dedicated followers result from leaders paying attention to their followers and their followers' needs. Clearly placing emphasis on the follower, servant leadership theory suggests communication, consideration, collaboration, trust, and ethics are critical considerations to serving followers. The theory emphasizes being a servant first, and in that role leading others out of service to them, rather than leading them for personal gain. Similar to exchange theory, the assumption in servant leadership is that when leaders focus on the needs and desires of their followers, those followers will then reciprocate through effective followership.

Finally, and as mentioned at the beginning of this book, is "authentic leadership" theory. Authentic leadership is about developing our own style, consistent with our unique attributes and character. With authentic leadership, we resist the organizational pressures to adhere to a specific style, or to emulate some exemplar's style, and instead we stay authentic to our core personality and character. The argument is that in doing so, we still adapt our style to evolving situational dynamics and in turn inspire authentic followership.[9]

So, the question remains: What is leadership? Or more specifically, what is *bona fide* leadership? Is it related to our deep-wired need to obey authority? Is it some inherent need for people to follow someone else in certain situations? If it is a need, then is it a source of power to be in a position to satisfy that need? What of those we would call leaders – do they have a need to be followed? If so, is that a source of power for followers to be in the position to satisfy that need? Indeed, could we say that followers need leaders, who in turn need followers? If so, is the leadership-followership arrangement based in trust? Is it a relationship? Does it function through social exchange? Are there specific roles that are played?

Perhaps bona fide leadership is best understood as a milieu. The word milieu is used to describe the surrounding social atmosphere in which people exist. A milieu, like a soup, contains many components and includes everything around and within a given social context. It can be a general attribute used to describe a surrounding or a set of occurrences that contribute to a social environment. A milieu is a social soup that is made up of people, emotions, attitudes, physical objects, and histories of interaction – essentially anything that is significant to social interaction within a given context.

Milieu paints the details of the social atmosphere, as well as the general sense of it. The term can pertain to any feature: physical, cultural, emotional, or any other quality. However it is used, the milieu of something conveys a general understanding of social context. As in social settings, a milieu is not meant to be definitive, rather it is a broad-brush term used to convey a general sense or impression. Bona fide leadership is a journey into the social milieu.

As previously mentioned, bona fide leaders need effective followers who need bona fide leaders. We can say that leadership does not exist without followers and that followership does not exist without leaders, so that implies that leadership defies a definition that would focus on just the leader or just the follower. Certainly, the characteristics and behaviors of those in a leadership position are important, but no more important than the characteristics and behaviors of those who choose to follow. Just as important as the leaders and followers, is the context. Leader and follower characteristics and behaviors play out against a backdrop of norms, expectations, values, perceptions, beliefs, needs, and desires.

Consider the John Kenneth Galbraith quote at the beginning of this chapter: "All of the great leaders have had one characteristic in common: it was the willingness to confront unequivocally the major anxiety of their people in their time. This, and not much else, is the essence of leadership."[2] This is the milieu, the willingness of someone to confront an anxiety shared by one or many, and their belief in the efficacy of that person to deliver them from that anxiety. This co-dependency is the essence of leadership. It is an SOS, a Save-Our-Ship, a distress signal that is sent out as a result of the anxiety. It also describes the leadership milieu.

The leadership milieu is a swirling combination of the characteristics, attributes, and behaviors of the leaders (Self), the same combination of characteristics, attributes, and behaviors of the followers (Others), and situational complexity that is creating the anxiety (Situation). Leadership defies a simple definition, common laws, or prescriptions and proscriptions for leader behavior. Every one of us is the perfect leader for some situation. There is an anxiety shared by others that we are perfectly equipped to address. When we face that SOS, we will need to understand who we are (introspection), who they are and how they interact with us (interspection), and how to make sense of and address the shared anxiety (perspective).

On Solitude

At an address to the plebe class at the United States Military Academy at West Point in 2009, William Deresiewicz, a former Associate Professor of English at Yale University delivered a message on the importance of solitude to leadership to the class.[10]

> Introspection means talking to yourself, and one of the best ways of talking to yourself is by talking to another person. Some other person you can trust, one other person to whom you can unfold your soul. One other person you feel safe enough with to allow you to acknowledge things—to acknowledge things to yourself—that you otherwise can't. Doubts you aren't supposed to have, questions you aren't supposed to ask. Feelings or opinions that would get you laughed at by the group or reprimanded by the authorities.

> How can you know [how to lead] unless you've taken counsel with yourself in solitude? I started by noting that solitude and leadership would seem to be contradictory things. But it seems to me that solitude is the very essence of leadership. The position of the leader is ultimately an intensely solitary, even intensely lonely one. However many people you may consult, you are the one who has to make the hard decisions. And at such moments, all you really have is yourself.

> If you want others to follow, learn to be alone with your thoughts.

Reflections

Is leadership a necessary word?

When are you ever alone?

What do you know about your leadership style?

What kind of follower are you?

What is meant by the phrase "leaders need followers need leaders"?

What kind of leader are you?

How do you know when you are a leader?

References

1. Blanchard, K.H. and S. Johnson, *The one minute manager*. 1st Morrow ed. ed. 1982, New York: Morrow.

2. Galbraith, J.K., *The age of uncertainty*. 1977, Boston: Houghton Mifflin.

3. Bolman, L.G. and T.E. Deal, *Reframing organizations*. 5. ed. ed. 2013, San Francisco, Calif: Jossey-Bass.

4. *Merriam-Webster Dictionary*. [cited 2019 Web Page]; Available from: https://www.merriam-webster.com/.

5. Carlyle, T., *On heroes, hero-worship and the heroic in history*. 1840, Chapman and Hall: London.

6. Galton, F., *Hereditary genius*. 2. ed. ed. 1892, London [u.a.]: Macmillian.

7. Spencer, H., *The study of sociology*. 1896, Appleton.

8. House, R.J. and R.N. Aditya, *The Social Scientific Study of Leadership: Quo Vadis?* Journal of Management, 1997. **23**(3): p. 409-473.

9. Avolio, B.J. and W.L. Gardner, *Authentic leadership development: Getting to the root of positive forms of leadership*. The Leadership Quarterly, 2005. **16**(3): p. 315-338.

10. Deresiewicz, W., *Solitude and Leadership*, in *The American Scholar*. 2010.

Epilogue

Bona Fide Leadership: A Hero's Journey

The privilege of a lifetime is being who you are.

A hero is someone who has given his or her life to something bigger than oneself.

The goal of life is to make your heartbeat match the beat of the universe, to match your nature with Nature.

Your sacred space is where you can find yourself again and again.

The big question is whether you are going to be able to say a hearty yes to your adventure

It is by going down into the abyss that we recover the treasures of life. Where you stumble, there lies your treasure.

—Joseph Campbell [1]

To illustrate how bona fide leaders are those who "answer the call" rather than "ring the bell" let's turn to a classic story-telling technique called "The Hero's Journey." The hero's journey is a common template used in telling stories about a protagonist who goes from a status quo existence to an adventure, rises to a significant challenge, and then returns to status quo changed or transformed. The hero's journey is widely taught as a technique in writing and literary classes. Originally presented by literature professor Joseph Campbell in 1949,[1] it consists of three acts: the *departure*, the hero leaves the ordinary world behind; the *initiation*, where the hero ventures into the unknown and is transformed through various trials and challenges; and the *return*, where the hero returns to the departure point in triumph and forever changed by the experience.

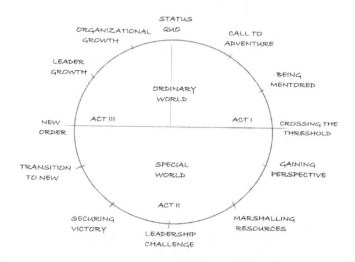

Figure 37: Based on Campbell's Hero's Journey

ACT I: DEPARTURE FROM ORDINARY WORLD

The hero's journey begins in the ordinary world. This is the status quo; the place where our future bona fide leader is an effective follower. This is our hero, the bona fide leader, only they do not know it yet. They are a critical thinker busy figuring out who they are, how to better understand others, and how to make sense of the situation that they are in. Their sensemaking has shaped what they "know." They are in the role of effective follower; a critical thinking, socially engaging, and loyal follower. They are also just one of the many people in the milieu.

They are in multiple role-sets, have developed many relationships, and have established trust across a range of people. Their social capital is solid and consists of a nice mix of bonding and bridging relationships. They read others well and can adjust their emotions to be situationally appropriate, they truly empathize with their colleagues and see them as more than just coworkers. They see them as friends, but also see them as being moms and dads, sons and daughters. They understand that their co-workers are so much more than the persona presented at work every day. They can read organizational nuance and have developed political savvy. This is their bona fide self, their ordinary.

The call to adventure (leadership) requires the hero to step away from the comfortable status quo. This is typically the result of a problem or challenge that can't be ignored. It is an imperative. Somebody needs to do something, it's an SOS. That something needs to be done is clear, but who will rise to the challenge?

Our bona fide leader might first refuse the call to action. They may be quite comfortable in the status quo. They are not necessarily looking to lead. It presents risks, requires leaving the comfortable status quo, it requires entering into new role-sets, building support, making tough decisions, and guiding followers through an unknown array of perils.

Our bona fide leader, compelled to serve, has accepted the call but they still hunger for perspective. From their vantage point in the ordinary world, there are some perspectives they are challenged to understand. Grounded by their own values, morals, and ethics, they look to experienced others to help them make sense of the broader context. They seek mentoring from someone who has that experience and that vantage point. The mentor provides insights, perspective, and social capital support. These mentors become an important source of sensemaking across all levels. Our bona fide leader emerges from Act I ready for the adventure.

ACT II: INITIATION INTO THE ADVENTURE

Now our bona fide leader is ready and committed to the challenge ahead. This is the moment where the bona fide leader steps out from the role of effective follower. In answering the call, they fundamentally change their role. Also, with this transition comes an entirely new range of role-sets, and each requires an investment. As these new role-sets are accommodated, our leader experiences role conflict as they struggle to make sense of the new challenge, its unmapped territory, and its new prescriptions and proscriptions for behavior. This can be the longest part of the hero's journey, as our bona fide leader seeks to find clarity and their place in the new order of things.

The leader is besieged with an entire new cast of characters. With each of these new characters, our leader must establish communication fidelity, credibility, trust, and relationships. They will meet supporters and detractors along the way and must see through the fog of competing agendas. They will learn new rules and rely on skills learned as an effective follower for interacting, communicating, and making decisions.

At some point the leader gains clarity as to just what the challenge is and perhaps how to best address it. The solution then becomes the ultimate goal – the quest. Yet before the leader calls for follower action, they prepare for the challenge. They prepare by marshalling support, building coalitions, amassing expertise and capability, building teams, and in general preparing the effective follower base to support the effort.

Our bona fide leader is now ready for action. They must confront the challenge, and if they survive it they will emerge the victor – transformed. This is a critical moment in the hero's journey because this becomes our leader's new sense. This is where our leader earns the title of leader. As our leader delivers us from the perils of the challenge, the benefits of meeting the challenge are now bestowed on the organization. For our leader, the reward is new-found knowledge or perspective. A leader's perspective.

ACT III: THE RETURN TO A NEW ORDINARY WORLD

Now that our bona fide leader has realized the reward, it is time to return to the ordinary world, but it will not be the same. There will be a new status quo. There will be consequences and new context in the aftermath of rising to the challenge. Previous relationships will be re-defined and new ones will be established. Reputations will be calibrated, role-sets will establish new norms in the form of prescriptions and proscriptions, and roles will shift. Power balances will shift and organizational politics will see new players and tactics.

But our leader is yet to be finished. They now face the final challenge, establishing the new normal, the new status quo. To fail at this is to risk failing the challenge. The change is not complete until it has been subsumed in the organization's culture. Legions of new-comers will be socialized into the new status quo as though it had always been so.

Finally, the hero's journey comes to an end and our leader returns home. However, they return forever changed. They've made new senses, have developed new perspectives, have grown and reshaped their social capital. They have a newly crafted reputation. For a bona fide leader, it is not so important to reap the rewards of meeting the challenge, as much as it is about how they conducted themselves in its pursuit. Were they able to uphold their values through the challenge? Were they able to honor the relationships and uphold the trust they started with? Were they able to "Save Our Ship?" Our bona fide leader, now settled into their new "ordinary world," stands ready for the next and perhaps greater call.

Perhaps more to the point, if we are consumed with trying to be something we're not, if we choose to be spectators rather than participants, or if we pursue perfection rather than possibilities, we will likely never begin the journey or enter the arena. It is in that arena and during the journey that leadership occurs.

In closing, consider the famous quote by Theodore Roosevelt during his *Citizenship in a Republic* in Paris, 1910.[2]

It is not the critic who counts; not the man who points out how the strong man stumbles, or where the doer of deeds could have done them better. The credit belongs to the man who is actually in the arena, whose face is marred by dust and sweat and blood; who strives valiantly; who errs, who comes short again and again, because there is no effort without error and shortcoming; but who does actually strive to do the deeds; who knows great enthusiasms, the great devotions; who spends himself in a worthy cause; who at the best knows in the end the triumph of high achievement, and who at the worst, if he fails, at least fails while daring greatly, so that his place shall never be with those cold and timid souls who neither know victory nor defeat.

References

1. Campbell, J., S.L. Brown, and P. Cousineau, *The hero's journey : the world of Joseph Campbell : Joseph Campbell on his life and work.* 1st ed. ed. 1990, San Francisco: Harper & Row.
2. Griggs, F.E., *Citizenship, Character, and Leadership: Guidance from the Words of Theodore Roosevelt.* Leadership & Management in Engineering, 2013. **13**(4): p. 230-248.

Made in USA - Crawfordsville, IN
22594_9781734850802
04.03.2020 1610